The Scorecard Killer : The True Story of Serial Killer Randy Kraft

Pete Dove

Published by Trellis Publishing, 2021.

THE SCORECARD KILLER : THE TRUE STORY OF SERIAL KILLER RANDY KRAFT

First edition. July 14, 2021.

ISBN: 979-8224558964

Written by Pete Dove.

THE SCORECARD KILLER : THE TRUE STORY OF SERIAL KILLER RANDY KRAFT

PETE DOVE

DR. HAROLD SHIPMAN

TAMI BARRERA

Dr. Harold Frederick Shipman was known in England as "Dr. Death." He is one of the most prolific serial killers in recorded history who, between 1974 and 1998, was suspected of killing over 215 of his patients by poisoning them with lethal injections of morphine. He was ultimately found guilty of 15 murders and sentenced to life in prison, never to be released. Shipman committed suicide while in prison on 13 January 2004.

Early Life

Born on 14 January 1946 in Nottingham, England, Harold Frederick Shipman, known as "Fred" or "Freddy", was the middle of Vera's and Harold Shipman Sr.'s three children. He had a sister Pauline who was seven years his senior and a brother Clive who was four years younger. His father was a lorry driver and his parents were devout Methodists. Shipman's childhood was far from normal thanks to his mother's influence; who instilled within him an early sense of superiority that served to taint his social relationships turning him into an isolated adolescent with few friends. According to a neighbor at the time, Shipman's mother was friendly but believed and acted as if her family was superior to everyone else. The neighbor also commented that Shipman was obviously his mother's favorite child; the one in whom she saw the greatest potential.

Vera dominated virtually every aspect of Shipman's life. She decided with whom he could play and when. She dictated what he wore and in order to distinguish him from the other children made him wear a tie even when his siblings were permitted more casual dress. In elementary school, Shipman was rather bright and performed reasonably well but his performance reduced to mediocrity when he reached higher levels. He was, however, determined to succeed and continued plodding along until he achieved his goal. This trait would follow him into adulthood when he had to retake his medical school entrance examinations after failing the first time.

There is much literature that suggests that Shipman had every opportunity to fit in and be part of a group. He was an accomplished football player and track runner; however, his air of superiority was his fundamental obstacle in cultivating meaningful friendships and other relationships with his peers. Throughout school—and even during medical school—his peers and teachers remarked that they barely remembered Shipman and those who did said that he often looked down upon them and seemed amused by the way his peers behaved. He was universally remembered as a loner even though he was far more sociable during medical school than his mother had ever permitted him to be. Such aloofness extended to his romantic relationships where nobody remembered Shipman ever having a girlfriend. In fact, he had taken his sister to school dances.

Shipman was especially close to his mother who died of lung cancer when he was just 17 years old. When she was first diagnosed, Shipman willingly cared for her and was fascinated with the effect morphine had on relieving her suffering. Her death would serve as the model for his subsequent modus operandi. During the last stages of her life, Vera's doctor made regular house calls and she was injected with morphine to ease her pain. Shipman repeatedly witnessed his mother's pain subside as a result of the morphine until she died on 21 June 1963. There is much speculation that his mother's death provided the impetus for his choice of career as a physician and his subsequent murderous spree.

In fact, the literature suggests that Shipman's behavior during the days leading up to her death closely paralleled what his behavior would be like as the most prolific serial killer in English history. Every day after school he would rush home, make his mother a cup of tea and sit and talk to her about his day. She looked very forward to this time; counting the minutes until he was home from school. Many suggest that this is where Shipman learned his endearing bedside manner that would make his patients adore him when he became a physician. When she was in severe pain—self-administration painkiller pumps had not been developed at this time—Vera's sole relief was courtesy of the family doctor. Shipman would watch in fascination as a shot of morphine had the tremendous power to alleviate his mother's distress. This image left an indelible mark on the impressionable 17-year-old who would later recreate it hundreds of time with his own patients.

Following her death Shipman was bound and determined to go to medical school. He was awarded a scholarship to the Leeds School of Medicine and graduated in 1970. Shortly thereafter he interned at Pontrefract General Infirmary in Pontrefract, West Riding of Yorkshire.

It was during this time he met his wife-to-be Primrose when he was 19. They married when she was 17 and already five months pregnant with their first child. Primrose's upbringing was eerily similar to Shipman's in that her mother restricted her friendships and controlled her behavior. Not a particularly attractive woman, she was, nevertheless, delighted to finally have a boyfriend.

In 1974—now a father of two—Shipman took a position as a general practitioner at the Abraham Ormerod Medical Centre in Todmorden, West Yorkshire. Interestingly, his hard work and enthusiasm enabled him to fit well into social circles. His senior colleagues—especially Dr. Michael Grieve—viewed him as a godsend who was able to keep them abreast of recent medical developments since he was fresh out of medical school.

Shipman started to suffer blackouts and he told his colleagues that he had epilepsy. His lies surfaced when the office receptionist, Marjorie Walker, found some disturbing entries in one of the druggist's controlled narcotics ledger. The records indicated that Shipman had been prescribing frequent and excessive amounts of pethidine—a synthetic form of morphine—in several patients' names. In a covert investigation by Dr. John Dacre, senior physician at the practice, proof that many of the patients on the ledger list neither required nor received the medication emerged.

When confronted with the discrepancy and the fact that the medication had found its way "into [Shipman's] very own veins" he first begged for a second chance and, when denied, became enraged, hurled a medical bag to the ground, threatened to resign, and stormed out. His colleagues were astounded at his violent and rather uncharacteristic behavior. Shortly thereafter, Shipman's wife stormed into the room where his peers were discussing how best to dismiss Shipman and, rather rudely, told them that her husband would never resign and that he would have to be forced out. One enduring question remained: did Shipman inject all of the stolen drugs into his own veins or had he already started killing his patients?

Shipman was fined £600 for forgery and attended The Retreat—a private drug rehabilitation clinic in York—for a brief time after being asked to leave his previous job. It is interesting to note that even after being fined for attempted forgery, Shipman's inflated self-image precluded him from realizing that his skill in this area was pathetic and that his ineptitude was easily exposed. This would be important when Shipman later attempted to forge one of his victim's signatures on a will. His unwavering arrogance and lack of judgment would contribute to his downfall.

After serving briefly as a medical officer for Hatfield College in Durham and doing some temporary work for the National Coal Board, Shipman became a general practitioner at the Donneybrook Medical Centre in Hyde, Greater Manchester in 1977. His colleagues trusted him; however, he had a reputation for being arrogant toward junior staff. Whereas today it would be unlikely that given his past Shipman would have been permitted to have access to controlled substances, at the time there were no restrictions and he was back in business. He was readily accepted by his colleagues and members of the community—yet another testament to his complete self-confidence and manipulative and persuasive demeanor.

Shipman did tell colleague Dr. Jeffery Moysey that he had had a problem with pethidine, had undergone treatment, and was now clean. He added that all Dr. Moysey could do was to trust and watch him for unusual or questionable behavior. Obviously, Shipman was not watched nearly closely enough.

Soon, Shipman reassumed his role as a dedicated, community-minded, hardworking physician and soon gained his patients' unwavering trust and his colleagues' respect; however, his subordinates repeatedly commented on his abusive and sarcastic persona which Shipman adeptly hid in front of those he wanted to impress.

Concerned about the unusually high rate of deaths and the curious similarities surrounding the condition of Shipman's patients at the time of their death—most were fully clothed and either sitting up in a chair or reclining in a settee fully clothed instead of in bed in their night clothes as was normally the case with elderly patients on their death beads—local undertaker Alan Massey questioned Shipman in March 1988 who told him that there was nothing to be concerned about. While Massey accepted Shipman at his word and took no further action, his daughter Debbie Brambroffe, also a funeral director, was not so easily assuaged. She approached Dr. Susan Booth who had also found the pattern disturbing. From a neighboring practice and pursuant to British law that required a doctor from an unrelated practice to countersign cremation forms issued by the original doctor, Dr. Booth was frequently called to Hyde funeral directors. These "witnesses" are then paid a fee for their service which many practitioners referred to as "cash for ash."

Dr. Booth shared her concerns with colleagues. One of them, Dr. Linda Reynolds of the Brook Surgery contacted coroner John Pollard who notified the police. Following a covert investigation that was highly questionable due to its seeming incompleteness, Shipman was cleared on the simple basis that his records seemed to be in order and authorities failed to contact the General Medical Council, or even check criminal records, which would have yielded evidence of his past record.

In 1983 Shipman was interviewed for the documentary World in Action about community treatment for the mentally ill and in 1993 Shipman—already a highly respected member of the community—founded his own surgery on Market Street.

The Crimes

Every one of Shipman's victims died from a fatal dose of morphine. A complete alphabetical list of all 215 people he murdered can be found at: http://www.theguardian.com/uk/2002/jul/19/shipman.health2.

The index case was Shipman's final victim before his arrest: former ceremonial Hyde Mayor Kathleen Grundy, an active and wealthy 81-year-old widow who was found dead in her house on 24 June 1998 when she failed to make an appearance at the Age Concern Club where she regularly served meals to elderly pensioners. When her friends and family went to check on her, Grundy was dead. They immediately called Shipman who had paid Grundy a visit mere hours earlier and was the last to see her alive. He claimed that the purpose of his visit was to take blood samples for a study on aging. Shipman pronounced Grundy dead and her daughter, Angela Woodruff, also a solicitor, was notified. Shipman told Woodruff that any postmortem examination was unnecessary seeing as how he had just seen her mother prior to her death.

After Grundy's burial, Woodruff received a troubling phone call from solicitors who claimed to have a copy of her mother's will. Since Woodruff's agency handled her mother's affairs she found this suspicious and examined the document that was so poorly typed that it made no sense and it contained a strange signature at the bottom. After initially thinking that Shipman may have been framed, she soon realized that he had killed her mother for profit and called the police.

Investigation

Investigation into Shipman's activities proved to be a long and arduous endeavor. As mentioned, Massey's daughter expressed concern regarding Shipman's patients that reached Dr. Reynolds who subsequently expressed her concerns to South Manchester District coroner John Pollard. Reynolds was particularly concerned about the large number of cremation forms for Shipman's elderly female patients which required countersignatures. She suspected Shipman of killing his patients but was not sure if this occurred through negligence or intent. The complaint ultimately reached Detective Superintendent Bernard Postles who took over the investigation and immediately determined the will to be a fake and began to look more closely at Shipman.

When police were first notified of the suspicions levied against Shipman, officers were unable to find sufficient evidence to warrant bringing charges against Shipman. After the fact when all of the evidence in the Shipman case was brought to light, police were blamed for assigning inexperienced officers to the case and subsequently abandoning the investigation. Later, The Shipman Inquiry uncovered that between the time police abandoned the investigation on 17 April 1998 and the time of Shipman's arrest, he had killed three more people; his last being Grundy. It was ultimately Grundy's daughter Woodruff whose personal investigation into her mother's death provided the impetus to fully scrutinize Shipman and learn the full extent of his murderous ways.

Woodruff became suspicious when solicitor Brian Burgess informed her about a will her mother had allegedly made that excluded Woodruff and her children but left £386,000 to Shipman. As her mother was always meticulous in her affairs, Woodruff seriously doubted that her mother had anything to do with the new will that superseded her previous one and could tell immediately that the signature on the will had been forged. At Burgess' urging, Woodruff reported her concerns about her suspicions into the forged will to the police who renewed their investigation.

Grundy's body had to be exhumed for examination. This was a very rare occurrence for British police as the majority of officers had never experienced one. They requested assistance from the National Crime Squad and Postles and crew would soon become uncomfortably unfamiliar with the process when they had to exhume 11 additional bodies of which eight were used in the criminal indictment. When Grundy's body was exhumed and examined it was found to contain traces of diamorphine. The medical examiner concluded that the deadly dose of morphine was administered within three hours prior to her death—exactly when Shipman had paid her a visit.

Following Shipman's arrest the typewriter on which the forged will was created was found in his house; along with medical records and an odd collection of jewelry. Further investigation into other deaths that Shipman had certified yielded a list of 15 cases that required further review and during this investigation the authorities discovered a pattern of Shipman administering lethal overdoses of diamorphine, signing his patients' death certificates, and then forging medical records to suggest that they had been in poor health which contributed to their deaths.

Further investigation generated additional troubling evidence. Shipman had urged the families of his patients to cremate their loved ones in inordinately large numbers while telling them that no further investigation of their deaths was necessary, even in those cases where the deceased had died of causes which were unknown to the families. If families pressed him for questions, Shipman would provide computer-generated medical notes that corroborated his cause of death determinations. Investigators would later discover that Shipman altered his medical notes shortly after killing his patients to ensure that his records matched the outcome. In Grundy's case Shipman had backdated and fabricated several entries in her medical records to give the impression that she was a morphine junkie.

Subsequent investigations began with those patients who had died following a Shipman house call and were not cremated because procurement of tissue samples for postmortem examination is easier. Several bodies were exhumed and examined. Next, police focused upon the cremated remains of other victims. Investigation into these victims was based primarily on preexisting known conditions, recorded causes of death, and the fact that Shipman was present shortly before they died.

Additional investigation into Shipman's forged computerized records was another area that provided considerable evidence that would be used against him at trial. When Shipman first encountered the computer he was technophobic but in true Shipman fashion soon declared himself to be an expert. However, he was not aware that the hard drive recorded to the second every phony alteration he made to a patient's records. In a taped interview between Shipman and the Greater Manchester Police when confronted with anomalies in his input of details Shipman claimed he did not recall doing whatever it was of which he was accused. Even when confronted with irrefutable computer evidence that he entered much data that was incorrectly dated and/or placed Shipman failed to acknowledge his actions.

Arrest and Trial

Shipman was arrested on 7 September 1998. His trial commenced on 5 October 1999 and was presided over by Mr. Justice Thayne Forbes. Shipman was charged with the murders of Marie West, Irene Turner, Lizzie Adams, Jean Lilley, Ivy Lomas, Murial Grimshaw, Marie Quinn, Kathleen Wagstaff, Bianka Pomfret, Norah Nuttall, Pamela Hillier, Maureen Ward, Winifred Mellor, Joan Melia, and Kathleen Grundy—all of whom had died between 1995 and 1998.

At the trial's outset Shipman's attorney, 46-year-old Nicola Davies who was predominantly a medical lawyer, presented three applications.

First, she alleged that the trial be postponed because she claimed that Shipman could not receive a fair trial because of the prior "inaccurate, misleading" coverage of his case in the media. Prosecutor Richard Henriques—one of the top barristers in all of Britain—countered that the reports alerted other families to potential irregularities regarding the death of their loved ones and was, therefore, beneficial.

Second, Davies wanted the court to hold three separate trials. She argued that the first should be Grundy's because hers was the only one that had a motive: greed. The second one, she argued, should only involve patients who were buried and exhumed because there was physical evidence of the morphine poising. Third, Davies argued that the last trial should cover those cremated due to the lack of physical evidence. Henriques asserted that the interrelated nature of the cases require that they not be severed to present a more comprehensive picture.

Davies' third application requested that evidence referred to in "volume eight" be disallowed during the trial. Volume eight detailed how Shipman acquired and hoarded morphine from 28 patients—many of whom had already died—in addition to continuing to write prescriptions for deceased patients—and keeping the medication for his own purpose. Further, he had prescribed opiates for a number of living patients who had never required strong painkillers such as morphine. After careful consideration, Justice Forbes denied each application. Proceedings were then adjourned until 11 October 1999 when the jury would be selected.

During the trial relatives of Shipman's victims testified and a clear pattern of Shipman's behavior was uncovered. He was portrayed as someone who demonstrated a lack of compassion, disregard for the wishes of his patients' relatives, and reluctance to even attempt to revive patients. Even more troublesome was that he would pretend to call emergency services in the presence of these relatives and then cancel the call when the patient turned out to be deceased. When telephone records were analyzed, Shipman had never made such calls. Additionally, the evidence demonstrated that Shipman hoarded drugs by falsely prescribing morphine to patients who didn't need it, over-prescribing it to others who did, and that he visited the homes of the recently deceased to pick up unused drug supplies for "disposal."

Victim Grundy's daughter Woodruff was an exceptional witness for the prosecution; giving detailed accounts of the conversations she had with Shipman, iterating how meticulous and detailed her mother was in all aspects of her life, talking about how much more in shape Grundy was at 81 than her children, among other compelling information. Similar accounts by other victims' family members would echo Woodruff's testimony; that their loved ones were healthy and that their deaths were suspicious.

Additional witnesses for the prosecution included computer analyst Detective Sergeant John Ashley regarding Shipman's doctoring of his medical records; calligraphy analyst Michael Allen who attested that Shipman's attempted signature forgery of Grundy was a pathetic attempt and, indeed, fraudulent; and pathologist Dr. John Rutherford who explained how the exhumation and subsequent examination on Shipman's victims was conducted, as well as the fact that the only fingerprints on Grundy's new will were those of Shipman and the two witnesses who signed the document—none belonging to the deceased.

During the second week of Shipman's trial his former colleagues and staff members testified. District nurse Marion Gilchrist described Shipman's reaction when he realized that he would soon be arrested. He allegedly stated that based upon the evidence authorities had he would be found guilty and that the only thing he did wrong was to not have Grundy cremated. Another of Shipman's patients issued a statement regarding what Shipman allegedly told her about Grundy's new will. He purportedly said that if he could bring her back he would because of all the trouble her death has caused and that he was going to say that he didn't want her money but because of all of his troubles he will get it and use some for philanthropic causes.

Finally, Shipman's former colleague Dr. Grenville testified as to how his actions would have been far different than Shipman's if he were in the same situation. Dr. Grenville said that instead of immediately pronouncing Grundy dead he would have carefully examined her body to ensure that death had, in fact, occurred, in addition to attempting to revive her in accordance with standard medical practice.

Evidence of Shipman's litany of lies continued. One glaring commonality was that when he "found" a patient dead he would pretend to call an ambulance. Such was the case with 77-year-old Lizzie Adams, a vibrant woman who enjoyed dancing with her partner William Catlow. Catlow had, in fact, stopped by to visit Adams on the day she died. He stated that he found Shipman examining her porcelain and crystal collection in the next room as Adams was dying nearby. Catlow testified that she felt warm and that he could feel her pulse. Shipman told him that was Catlow's own pulse and that she had already expired.

Similarly, in the case of Nora Nuttall, her son Anthony testified how he had left his mother alone at home for only 20 minutes and when he returned he found Shipman leaving their house. Shipman allegedly told Anthony that he just called for an ambulance. When Anthony went to his mother she looked asleep but he could not revive her. Soon after, Shipman barely touched her neck and said that he was sorry but she was gone. When Nuttall's sister went to Shipman's office for details of her sister's death, Shipman fabricated lies of how Nuttall called him to say that she was ill and when he was paged he just happened to be in the area and stopped by. When telephone records proved him wrong, Shipman invented a new lie.

Ultimately, the lie regarding his collecting blood from Grundy for some study took the cake. Shipman initially testified that the blood samples had gone for analysis; however, when the prosecution proved that there was no study on aging Shipman suddenly "remembered" that he had left the samples under some notes and when he discovered them they were no longer useful and, thus, he disposed of them.

The myriad lies coupled with Shipman's haughty and arrogant attitude throughout the trial certainly didn't substantiate the defense's attempt to portray him as an old-fashioned caring and dedicated physician who would go out of his way to help his patients. Compounding the problem was that he kept changing his story during questioning.

Additional testimony revealed Shipman to have an utter lack of compassion with respect to announcing his patients' deaths to loved ones; oftentimes being vague enough to make them guess and then berating them for "not listening" to him carefully enough. He even called the neighbor of one of his victims stupid when she confronted him returning to her neighbor's—Gloria Ellis—house and had asked him if Ellis had suffered a stroke. The witness stated that she believed Shipman to be an insurance man instead of a doctor.

One final example of Shipman's callousness occurred when Detective Sergeant Philip Reade visited Shipman's office to locate the next of kin of one Ivy Lomas who was Shipman's only patient to die in his office. Reade said that Shipman was laughing and said that she was "such a nuisance that he was having part of the seating area permanently reserved for Ivy with a plaque to the effect—seat permanently reserved for Ivy Lomas" and that while she "could have taken her last breath" Shipman was busy seeing other patients and made no effort to resuscitate her. Dr. Grenville told the court that the Lomas situation was a medical emergency to which he would have given his complete attention.

In Shipman's defense, Davies had asked the forensic analyst about the validity of testing postmortem tissue for drugs and whether his finding of morphine was proof of single or multiple doses. The scientist said that he couldn't say; however, American pathologist Dr. Karch

Steven took the stand and explained the relatively new technique of analyzing hair samples for evidence of ongoing drug use and that in every single case none of Shipman's victims were long-term morphine users.

Shipman also lied about carrying morphine and this lie came back to bite him. After killing his patients he would collect their morphine supplies—which were often overprescribed—for his own "stash." In one case, Jim King was incorrectly diagnosed as having cancer and Shipman treated him with copious amounts of morphine. When King's condition worsened Shipman went to King's house and told him that he needed to give him an injection. King's wife was wary since King's aunt and father had both died after a Shipman visit and she told Shipman that he could write out a prescription. She said that he became increasingly arrogant and snotty.

When the case was ready to go to the jury it took Justice Forbes two weeks to separate all of the evidence presented and to caution jurors that there were no witnesses who saw Shipman kill anyone and to utilize common sense and not react to the anger, disapproval, disgust, or sympathy they had likely felt during the trial. On 31 January 2000 at 4:43 p.m. following six days of deliberation the jury found Shipman guilty of killing 15 patients via lethally injection of diamorphine, and one count of forging Grundy's will. He was sentenced to 15 consecutive life sentences—plus four years for the forgery—and Justice Forbes recommended that Shipman never be released which was later upheld by Home Secretary David Blunkett. Interestingly, this recommendation occurred just a few months prior to Parliament's stripping British government ministers of their power to set minimum terms for convicted offenders.

Shipman never displayed any emotion when the verdict was read. Neither did his wife.

Shipman became the only British doctor in the country's legal history to be found guilty of murdering his patients. While a number of other instances could have been tried, authorities concluded that it would have been difficult for Shipman to have received a fair trial in light of the substantial publicity surrounding his original trial; not to mention that further trials would have been moot given his sentence. Ultimately, The Shipman Inquiry estimated the number of Shipman's victims to be as many as 250.

The General Medical Council stripped Shipman of his medical license on 11 February 2000.

Many of his former patients continue to struggle with the possibility that they could have been next and say they owe their lives to Angela Woodruff whose determination to get to the bottom of her mother's suspicious death proved to be Shipman's ultimate demise.

Death

Shipman consistently denied his guilt by disputing the plethora of scientific evidence against him but failed to offer any statements regarding his actions. His wife was also in denial. A number of scientific inquiries were launched in attempts to determine the true extent of Shipman's murderous ways. During these investigations Shipman was incarcerated first in Durham Prison and was transferred to Wakefield Prison in June 2003 to be closer to his family.

Shipman committed suicide at 6:20 p.m. on 13 January 2004, the eve of his 58th birthday, and was pronounced dead at 8:10 p.m. Shipman had hanged himself with bed sheets from the window bars of his cell. Whereas British tabloids expressed joy at his death—as evidenced by a celebratory front-page headline in The Sun that said, "Ship Ship hooray," his victims' families stated that they had felt cheated that they would never have the satisfaction of knowing why Shipman did what he did or to hear a confession. Others dubbed him a "cold coward" and condemned the Prison Service for allowing his suicide to occur. Other publications pushed for investigation into the state of Britain's prisons and the welfare of their inmates with some wanting sentencing reform.

Shipman's motive for his suicide was never established although he had reportedly told his probation officer that doing so would ensure that his widow could receive a National Health Service pension and lump sum. In fact, she did receive a full National Health Service pension which would not have occurred had Shipman died after age 60. Further, there continues to be speculation as to when Shipman began killing his patients as well as the exact number of people who died by his hand.

Aftermath

A number of audits and inquiries into Shipman's patients occurred. A clinical audit conducted by University of Leicester Professor Richard Baker examined the number and pattern of deaths of Shipman's patients and compared this figure with similar records from other health care practitioners. Baker found that the rate of death among Shipman's elderly patients was considerably higher, were clustered at certain times of the day, and that Shipman was present in an inordinately high number of cases. Baker's audit estimated that Shipman was likely responsible for at least 236 patient deaths over 24 years.

In January 2001 senior West Yorkshire detective Chris Gregg was directed to lead an investigation into 22 deaths in his jurisdiction in which Shipman was involved. When the results were submitted in July 2002 it was purported that Shipman had killed at least 215 of his patients between 1975 and 1998 in Todmorden, West Yorkshire, and Hyde.

In a separate inquiry commission chaired by High Court Judge Dame Janet Smith, 500 of Shipman's patients' records were examined and a 2,000-page report concluded that it was highly likely that Shipman murdered at least 218 of his patients with a number of additional suspicious deaths which could not be positively attributed to Shipman. One of them, 67-year-old Margaret Thompson died in March 1971, shortly after Shipman obtained his medical license, while recovering from a stroke and she is widely believed to be Shipman's first victim. Other potential victims during his early years practicing medicine have never been officially proven.

The majority of Shipman's victims were elderly women who adored their doctor, lived alone and, consequently, were vulnerable. They were in good health before they died. On 24 January 2005, in her sixth report, Smith stated that she believed that Shipman had likely killed seven more patients including a four-year-old girl when Shipman was in the early stages of his career at Pontrefract General Hospital. She increased her estimation to 250; however, because 459 people died while under his care the exact number of victims is unknown.

Shipman's motive for killing is also unknown. As is the case with most serial killers there is usually some motive, some toying with victims to reinforce their power over them, or some smoking gun but all of Shipman's victims died peacefully and all but one did so in the comfort of their own homes. Some speculation asserts that he hated older women and thought that the elderly were a drain on the health care system while others believed he was simply recreating his own mother's death to satisfy some sort of need. The majority, however, believe that Shipman's own self-perceived superiority made him believe that he could do whatever he wanted without fear of apprehension despite that he had been caught for forging prescriptions years ago.

At Smith's urging in The Shipman Report, the General Medical Council charged six additional physicians who signed cremation forms for some of Shipman's victims with misconduct, alleging that they should have noticed a pattern between Shipman's house calls and his patients' deaths. These physicians were acquitted.

A 2005 inquiry into Shipman's suicide alleged that it could not have been predicted or prevented but that the prison procedures should be reexamined.

Also in 2005 Shipman was suspected of having stolen some of his victims' jewelry as over £10,000 worth had been found in his garage in 1998. Despite Shipman's widow urging for it to be returned to her the police notified Shipman's victims' families asking them whether they could identify it.

On 30 July 2005 in Hyde Park, the Garden of Tranquility was opened as a memorial garden to Shipman's victims. As of 2009 many of his victims' families are seeking compensation for the loss of their loved ones.

RANDY KRAFT

California in the 1970s. Serial Killer central. Over a hundred bodies turned up, murdered, mutilated, assaulted in less than a decade. And at least two thirds of them were the result of just one man – compulsive killer Randy Kraft.

It is believed that there were at least three serial killers operating in the south western state at that time, possibly more, but Kraft was by far the most prolific.

On the night of May 14th, 1983 Sgt Michael Howard was on late night patrol. He and his partner were cruising the highway when they noticed a Toyota Celica driving erratically. It was trying to stay in its lane, but failing badly.

Sgt Howard put on the patrol car's red and blue flashing lights, but the Celica did not pull over. It continued on its way for several more minutes before finally easing to one side, so close to the barrier that the passenger door could not be opened. Howard got out of the patrol car and approached the stopped vehicle, and as he did so the driver's side door opened, and out stepped a moustachioed man in his thirties.

The policeman immediately realised this was going to be no routine case of driving under the influence because the suspect was displaying some very strange behaviour. But had Howard known then what he came to understand later, he would not have been surprised by the oddities with which he was now confronted. Because the man lurching before him was Randy Stephen Kraft. And he was acting under that part of his personality which came to the fore when compulsion became his driving force. A compulsion to kill.

The driver held a beer bottle in his hand, which he immediately smashed to the floor. Not, it seemed, to create a home made weapon, but to use the smell of beer that permeated the night to disguise the fact that he had been drinking.

If the beer bottle was immediately obvious, then so was the fact that Kraft was drunk. He could not pass any of the standard inebriation tests used in those days, such as walking in a straight line. It was at this point that Howard noticed the driver's pants were undone and open.

Kraft was cuffed, and inserted in the back of the patrol vehicle. Meanwhile Howard approached the Celica. Inside, he was met with a disturbing sight. A young man was sitting slouched over. A jacket was placed over his lap, and there were strangulation marks around his neck. When the jacket was removed, it became apparent that some kind of sexual activity had taken place. The victim's pants and underwear were down, and something had been wedged beneath him to thrust his genitalia upwards. Also in the Celica was the detritus of alcohol and drug use, including a bottle that had recently contained a powerful tranquiliser.

Inside the patrol car, Howard recalls the man they had arrested frequently asking 'How is my friend?' The answer though was clear. That friend was dead. Despite desperate efforts to resuscitate him, he was beyond the help of emergency aid. The man was Terry Lee Gambrel, a twenty five year old marine stationed nearby. He had set out than night to hitchhike to a party, but had picked the wrong car in which to travel.

The next morning Orange County forensics officer Jimmy White was called to inspect the Toyota. The brown Celica was a mess. Everything from papers to pine cones was littered inside. But it was in the boot that White and his team hit their first jackpot. 'I did find a notebook,' recalls the forensic expert.

Michael Howard remembers the event. 'The book was full of codes and initials and numbers. It was like some kind of code book,' he said. That list was seemingly meaningless and random. Words such as 'Deodorant' appeared above 'dog'. Then 'Teen trucker' removed any kind of suggestion that there was an alphabetical order to the contents of the page. 'M.C. Laguna', 'Lakes me', '7th Street'... for every seemingly definable terms, such as 'Iowa' or 'parking lot' others such as 'navy white' or 'user' confused the issue.

Therefore, as clear as it was that the list was important, officers could not decipher it. 'It was a list, a list of descriptions, people or places. It certainly seemed to be important,' said Jimmy White. It seemed as though this could also be a list of potential victims. If so, the sixty plus terms on the page could indicate that police had a major serial killer on their hands.

California was in the midst of a long plague of unsolved murders. Patterns had emerged from the more than a hundred bodies that had been found in the southern part of the state over the previous decade. The majority were discovered close to freeways. Often, the victims had consumed alcohol and drugs – sometimes a fatal amount of these. Disturbingly, some had been discovered with foreign objects stuffed into their rectums.

Michael Howard wondered if he had stumbled upon the serial killer, or at least one of them, for which the authorities had been searching for years. 'I just thought we were lucky to have stumbled on this. We were fortunate to be in the right place at the right time,' he reflected.

Meanwhile, the search of Kraft's brown and untidy Celica was continuing. Jimmy White soon made another discovery. Underneath a car mat was a tucked a brown envelope. It contained forty seven photographs. One in particular stood out. The photo shows a young man face down on a gold, velour sofa. He is spread-eagled on the cushions, and apparently dead. Others too displayed inanimate, probably dead, bodies.

Further searches of the car reveals incriminating evidence after suspicious sign. For example, the front seats are soaked with dried blood, but the body of Gambril has no wounds. It is clear that this vehicle has carried other seriously injured, or dead, passengers.

The secret to discovering whether Kraft was a mass murderer lay, it was clear, in the undecipherable notes scrawled on a page of a notebook. Police in Orange County made the thoughtful decision to pass details on to officers searching for killers elsewhere in the state – there were plenty at that time – and attempts to interpret the words intensified. The page started to become known as the 'scorecard', and Kraft was given the pseudonym of the Scorecard Killer.

Officers studied the scorecard endlessly, and eventually, slowly, painfully words began to make sense. Police re-examined their case notes of investigations running back more than a decade to the early 1970s. Sometimes further still... then, finally, a breakthrough was made. Number three on the list of random terms, letters and numbers were the initials EDM.

In 1972 a young marine had gone missing. His name was Edward Moore, and his middle name was Daniel. EDM seemed to make sense. Clearly, their suspicions that the list was some kind of macabre tally of victims were gaining legitimacy. A trawl through records showed that ten marines had gone missing in the region over the previous ten years. Now it was time to link their disappearances with the clues on the list. Suddenly, 'navy white' might make sense. As could 'marine down' and 'marine Carsan.' What had seemed a totally random collection of letters and numbers now screamed out at the officers investigating the case.

Julie Haney is a retired cold case investigator who worked for the authorities in California. She explained how the marines would have been socialising at the weekends. They would often hitchhike to get around. That was a popular activity in the 1970s, such an innocent time before young people fully realised the risks that they were putting themselves under by getting into a car or truck with a complete stranger. Marine Roger Dickerson, who was just eighteen, was found on the beautiful Laguna Beach in 1974. He had been sodomised, strangled and bitten on the nipple and genitals. Police felt that he could be the MC Laguna on the list. Many others of the bodies discovered over the years had also been bitten; this is a common, primeval sexual drive and when not consensual, is indicative of a need to dominate a partner.

As links started to come to the fore the question was raised as to why the authorities had not made better progress with their investigations over the past ten or twelve years. The reasons became clear, but not justifiable. Firstly, different forces enjoyed their empires. Handing over a juicy case to another department was not in their DNA, and so information which might have helped to find Kraft before he committed so many offences remained scattered over the different offices in California. Secondly, the victims were all young males. Many of them were homosexuals, or suspected of having a sexual orientation which, even in liberal California, was not fully accepted. Especially, it has to be said, behind the conservative doors of local police stations. As a result, the murders were never seen as high enough profile to trigger a determined and resilient police investigation. The thought too often remained that these were young men who partly deserved what they got, because of the lifestyle in which they participated.

XXXXXXX

Severely anti-social behaviour in adulthood can often be traced back to traumatic childhood experiences. But in the case of Randy Kraft, that does not seem to be the case. He was born on March 19th 1945 in Long Beach, California. The Kraft family were not wealthy by any means, but they scraped together a living. Home might be a converted army hut, adapted into a wooden three bedroomed house by Randy's father, but it was still a home. Luxuries might be rare, but Randy's mother worked extra jobs to put food on the table. And although the boy's relationship with his father was distant, there is no evidence at all that it was abusive or violent in any way. It seems as though his relations with his mother and siblings were good.

In fact, his mother was a doting figure in his life, as though she sought to compensate for his less interested father. Criminal Psychologist David Holmes is familiar with this kind of family set up. They create an environment, he says, where 'children strive for success, or attention.' Young people in this type of family arrangement often make a lot of their lives, because they become driven by a need for recognition. Such success is, of course, often very much on the surface. Deeper down, they are frequently people whose sense of dissatisfaction that something is missing from their lives is never properly addressed.

That striving does not always take the form of something regarded by society as appropriate or worthwhile. 'This is often the background of serial killers,' explains Holmes.

Kraft's school days seem to reflect the typical outcomes of this type of family. He was a successful student, graduating tenth out of his class of 390. Kraft was also a popular boy at school, one who was hard working and respected. He knew from sometime in High School that he was homosexual, but tried dating girls, although the experiences were not good for him. However, nothing has come to light about his childhood years that suggests anything other than normal adolescent behaviour.

That changed when Kraft was twenty one. Prior to that, the young man had come out to his parents. Unsurprisingly, his father was horrified by the announcement, but although his mother was disappointed, she was understanding. Kraft had tried a subtle way of preparing his family for the news that their son was gay. He had taken a succession of young men home with him, but apparently both parents were oblivious to the hints.

Still, after coming out he maintained a good, if slightly more distant relationship with his parents and sisters.

Matters began to go downhill when Kraft was caught in a sting operation. He was arrested for lewd behaviour after propositioning a plain clothed policeman who was seeking to entrap homosexual people in a park they often frequented. However, as it was Kraft's first 'offence' he was let off without charge.

Meanwhile, the young man was getting seriously into politics. Classmates described him as 'somewhere right of Attila the Hun', but in his ultra-conservative home town of Westminster, Orange County, such views were commonplace.

However, as he hit his twenties Kraft's political views took a sudden turn. Perhaps because he recognised the narrow minded nature of conservative views towards homosexuality, he suddenly signed up as a Democrat. He was such an avid supporter and helper on Bobby Kennedy's campaign of 1968 that he received a personal letter of thanks from the senator.

XXXXX

Shortly after graduating from college Kraft joined the air force. He was a promising airman, quickly earning advanced security clearance and being promoted to a rank of Airman First Class. Kraft was an obsessively hard worker, and his superiors were impressed. But after a year in service, the young recruit effectively signed his own exit papers. He reported to a senior officer that the was homosexual. Such an admission meant discharge, and the air force listed this as for 'medical reasons.' Kraft, it seemed, wanted a more honest explanation of his expulsion, and even sought legal support to achieve this. But he was many years ahead of his time, and the air force refused to change the wording on his discharge papers. By now it was July 1969, and Kraft had just turned twenty four years old.

On discharge, he took a job as a barman at a gay bar on Sunset Beach. He embraced the gay lifestyle that flourished there.

Matters started to deteriorate with the distasteful case of a thirteen year old runaway by the name of Joey Francher. It was March 1970. The boy, who later frecamed a biker, was a vulnerable kid who seemed confident on the surface. Kraft met him by chance, on Huntingdon Pier, and offered the youngster a cigarette. The two began to talk and realising the child had nowhere to stay, Kraft offered him a room in his own flat. Francher leapt at the chance, no doubt terrified about what might happen to him if he spent the night on the Californian streets.

But once back at his flat, Kraft plied the young boy with alcohol and drugs, and showed him pornography. As the cocktail of diazepam and alcohol began to take effect on the youngster's mind, Kraft sexually assaulted him. The next morning, he headed off for work as usual, almost as though he saw neither risk nor wrong in what he had done. Francher then fled from the flat and made his way to the local police station. He reported some of what had happened – missing out the part about being raped by the older man - and police went to investigate. A catalogue of mistakes then occurred which, with hindsight, wasted a chance to stop Kraft before his criminality escalated. Better police practice might have saved the lives of nearly seventy boys and young men (possibly many more). But times and standards were different in 1970.

Firstly, it seems as though police failed to recognise the seriousness of the sexual assault on Francher. No alarm bells were raised by the fact the boy was distressed, that pornography was littered around the flat or that the boy had fled the apartment in his bare feet. They were more interested in the drugs he had taken. When he admitted that he had accepted these freely, they decided that there were no charges that they could bring. However, by then they had searched Kraft's flat without obtaining a warrant. Such activity prevented them from using any evidence they found should they subsequently decide that Kraft could be charged.

Vonda Pelto was a counsellor and clinical psychologist who worked in the county men's jail at the time Kraft was finally arrested. She sees nothing unusual in Francher's reluctance to report the rape he had suffered. In fact, she describes that as 'normal' behaviour from young boys, who are often embarrassed by what they have been put through. That should not, however, have prevented the police from making sensitive enquiries.

Seeking to do something useful with his life, Kraft enrolled at Long Beach State University, where he studied for a teaching qualification. It was there that he met Jeff Graves. It seems that in many ways Kraft was comfortable with his sexuality and his steady relationship with his new boyfriend. However, below the surface bubbles of the deviant behaviour that would soon burst forth from him were beginning to surface. It was around this time that Kraft committed, almost certainly, his first murder.

Wayne Dukette was thirty. His body was found near the Ortega Highway on October 5th 1971; he had been missing since late September. His body was already putrefying, and police had initially put the bartender's death down to acute alcohol poisoning. However, when the scorecard began to make sense as a list of victims, the first word on it was 'Stable'. The Stable was a gay bar on Sunset Beach. It was also the bar in which Dukette worked.

Over the next ten years Kraft's offending behaviour began to take on a familiar routine. He would meet gay men, sometimes they were very young, just in their early twenties or even teens. He took them back to his flat, where he would drug them. It seems as though his victims were usually willing participants in this part of his murderous schemes. Then he would assault them, strangle them and often photograph their dead bodies. Next, they would be hauled into his car, and dropped beside some highway.

Not all of the men Kraft took back home became victims, but somewhere up to a hundred of them did.

Carrying around photographs of his victims, as Kraft did, seems an astonishingly risky behaviour to follow. However, David Holmes has a theory as to why the intelligent man took this chance. 'He was really obsessive,' the psychologist explained. 'He couldn't let go. The images, the experiences, in some way it maintained his control over his victims, to be able to look through the photographs and revisit the experiences and relive them.

As is often the case with psychopathic killers, Kraft's crimes showed an increasing level of violence and mutilation. Special Officer Julie Haney explained that he began to torture his victims before he killed them. He would keep them alive for days, and sexually molest them. His offending became even more bizarre. His victims would have objects inserted into their rectum, and their genitals would be hacked off.

Mark Hall was another victim. On January 3rd 1976 his mutilated body was discovered. Hall's eyelids had been cut off - experts deduced that this was so Hall was forced to watch what was being done to him. Then, a car cigarette lighter was used to burn various parts of his body. But Kraft's perverse behaviour did not stop there. Next he inserted a round topped cocktail stick into the victim's penis, before forcing that into his anus. Hall was recorded on the score card as 'New Year's Eve.' Other bodies found during this stage of his offending were castrated, it was as though he was emasculating his victims.

It was, according to David Holmes, like he was trying to turn his victims into females.

The year before Hall's discovery, Kraft experienced his closest shave with police to date. It was 1975 and Kraft had already killed fourteen times when he came across a group of four teenage boys in a parking lot outside the Ripples gay bar. He engaged the boys in conversation, and told them that he had beer in his car. Keith Cropwell and Kent May made the foolish decision to get into the stranger's Mustang. Kraft immediately began to dish out beer, all the better to wash down the Valium pills he was also willing to supply. Soon, the boys were semi-conscious. He decided to drop one of them, Kent May, back at the Ripples parking lot, presumably so that he could be alone with Cropwell.

A month later Cropwell's severed head was found in a nearby by lake. But this time Kraft has made an error. His car, the brightly coloured Mustang, is not the sort of vehicle commonly seen on the roads of California. With the description of it from the boys, police link it to Randy Kraft, but his boyfriend provides an alibi. The police show no further interest in the killer.

As for the scorecard, Cropwell's murder is listed under the cryptic term, 'parking lot'. With hindsight, the identification is easy to decode, but without the clue of a boy picked up from such a place, the term was meaningless to police.

A part of the reason that Kraft was able to avoid detection was that he was, to everybody who was not a victim, a perfectly normal person. Friendly and intelligent, nobody would suspect him of being a serial killer.

XXXXX

Kraft's crimes were defined by control and denial. The killings were brutal in the extreme, but also cold and calculating. When his case came to trial on 26th September 1988, Orange County was about to hold one the longest, most expensive and most horrific trials in the history of Californian courts.

It seemed, from the scorecard, that he had definitely killed at least sixty eight men and boys. Police feared that the number could be as high as one hundred. They could tie him clearly to forty of the murders of young males that had polluted the streets of the Pacific state since the turn of the 1970s. However, they decided to bring just sixteen homicides to trial (alongside one case of sodomy and one of emasculation.) These were cases where evidence was strongest; they would be enough to secure the death penalty for the sadistic killer.

A part of Kraft's psychotic personality saw him hold an astonishingly narcissistic view towards himself. He saw the court as a mere inconvenience, something too low to cast judgement on his actions. He felt he could walk over the evidence as required. But he underestimated the strength of the cases against him.

One of these in particular stood out. Once more, Jimmy White was the forensic officer who worked the murder. Near Seal Beach was found the body of Eric Church. He was discovered wearing purple socks, and fibres from the socks were discovered in Kraft's car. But even with this damning evidence, the killer was not concerned. He smiled as each revelation was cast before the jury. It is as though he believed that the court would be simply unable to convict him. He treated his trial like an amusing but slightly annoying interruption to his life. He was wrong. After eleven days of deliberation the jury found him guilty of every homicide for which he was tried.

'Briefly I would like to say that I have not murdered anyone, and I believe that any reasonable review of the record will show that. That is all I have to say.' And with those words Kraft closed his account of an astonishing reign of terror.

But if it seemed as though he had moved on in his mind, police were left with numerous unsolved cases which they believed, confidently, lay at the door of this mass murderer. Yet they could not prove it.

As recently as 2012 Julie Haney was charged with looking back at some of the murders it is believed that Kraft committed. Some were by now forty years old, or more. Specifically, she was asked to investigate a body found back in the 1970s but never identified. The body had a distinctive military haircut, and a search through military records suggested that the man could be Oral Stuart, who had gone missing at around the same time that the body was found.

Stuart's parents were still alive, and were able to confirm that, after so long, their son had been found. Perhaps there was some comfort for them in that, or closure at least. Although, that the military man's body was discovered naked, with bite marks on his neck, would have been the cause of considerable distress, even after such a long time had passed.

Oral Stuart's injuries fitted with those found on other victims of Kraft. Although he denied involvement in the soldier's death, on the scorecard one of the unidentified links was simply called Iowa. Stuart hailed from this state. It seems as though another victim of the sadistic mass murderer had been found.

Today, Kraft is an old man. He continues to sit on death row, but age has not mellowed him. He refuses to offer any comfort to family members of the dead by either admitting to being responsible for their loved one's demise, or offering any information about how it may have occurred. It is as though to speak about the crimes would break the seal of denial he has built up around himself, and make him lose control over those events.

But that psychosis which defines him is of no comfort to the surviving families of many young men who died violently in a frenzy of sexual deviation in 1970s California. Julia Haney sums up the killer neatly. She says:

'I had never met anybody, prior to Randy Kraft, that literally has no soul.'

KILLER NURSE :

THE TRUE STORY OF GENENE JONES

34

KORI MAYER

Genene Anne Jones was born on July 13th, 1950 in Texas but was given up for adoption. Her adopted parents had three other children. Two were older and one was younger than Genene.

EARLY LIFE

Her adopted parents were Richard and Gladys Jones. Richard, better known as "Dick", a night club and was a gambler. He was a big spender and generous when he was flush. His club was called the Kit Kat Swim Club, the place had a dance floor with a patio and pool outside. His wife Gladys was the disc jockey at the club and the couple lived an extravagant lifestyle. They had a mansion that looked down on San Antonio, would travel often and they would both have pilot licenses .

At the age of ten, however, Genene's father was arrested for stealing the safe of a customer who had been at Jones' club at the time of the robbery. These charges were later dropped.

It could have been due to intimidation on Dick's part. The man was six feet tall, weighed a solid 240 pounds and was bold. He had an aggressive demeanor when needed and his adopted daughter developed the same traits.

His business soon failed, however. The shady Kit Kat Club soon turned into a family themed restaurant which put Dick further into debt. He then sold off the restaurant and earned a living putting up billboards around San Antonio. Genene would later describe helping her father put up the billboards as one of the happier times of her life.

Still, Genene felt as if she suffered from neglect in the adopted home. The parents had paired off the four kids on the basis of age. Genene had an older brother Wiley and an older sister named Lisa. She had a younger brother named Travis who had a learning disability that she doted on and cared for. Nonetheless, she felt jealous of all the attention that Lisa would receive. Genene referred to herself as the "black sheep" of the family and took out her frustrations on her classmates at school. She worked in the library at John Marshall and was described as "kind of bossy" by the high school librarian as she would berate other student volunteers who weren't doing their jobs up to her standards. Short and chubby, Genene felt unattractive and began to become known for lying and manipulating people.

"Lying was like talking for her," one of her classmates recalled as Genene would often tell people that she was related to Micky Dolenz, the band member of the Monkees, and that she would routinely have phone conversations with him all the time.

Tragedy would strike in her teens, however, when her younger brother Travis died in a freak accident.

He had put together a pipe bomb which exploded in his face, sending metal shards into his head. Genene took the loss hard, arriving at the funeral with a large flower wreath, crying hysterically, then feinting.

"You wonder when Genene's mind got twisted," forensic psychologist Dina Foster said. "It had to have been early on in her development when somehow, someway she got a surge of power when she was care taking for someone particularly a child. This was probably her brother, Travis. Being a caregiver for him made her feel important. She realized that she could be respected and have people look up to her until it became twisted."

A year later, her father died of cancer at the age of 56 which further devastated Genene. She had yet to graduate high school and wanted to get married. Her adopted mother refused as she Genene's choice of mate, a dropout named James "Jimmy" Harvey Delany Jr as nothing but trouble.

The two would marry, however, and live in a guesthouse near the mansion. Jimmy, however, was only interested in cars and drinking. The two would squabble often until Jimmy decided to join the Navy. With her husband away a basic training, Genene would not remain faithful, going after both single and married men. She had an affair with the newlywed husband of a former high school classmate. Then she began to tell people she had been sexually abused as a child. After four years of marriage, Genene divorced Jimmy as she stated that he had been physically abusive toward her.

Genene would threaten divorce but the two would reconcile.

"She experienced abandonment twice," Foster said. "The first go around was when her mother gave her up for adoption. The second go around was when her brothers and father died back to back. She had lost two loved ones to illnesses and one to a tragic accident. She felt helpless and out of control. But unlike most people, Genene went the criminal route in order to assuage the pain. She had to do things to get the power and control back."

CAREER LIFE & DIVORCE

Genene entered Mim's Beauty School and became a beautician, finding work at the Methodist Hospital beauty parlor. She had her first child, Richard, in 1972 while she and Jimmy were stationed in Georgia. They would move back to San Antonio but by that time the marriage was failing. She filed for divorce in Bexar County, eight months after Richard was born and stated that her husband was "a man of violent and ungovernable temper and passion" while also accusing him of "unconscionable brutality and physical cruelty." She won a court order that forbade her husband from going near both her or baby Richard. Two months later, however, the couple had gotten back together and the judge threw out the divorce suit.

"Clearly they had an on and off again relationship," Foster said. "Jimmy was hapless, wanting to do nothing more than race cars and party. So in some aspects Genene had found her soul mate, a man who needed taking care of."

But on June 3rd, 1974, Genene filed for divorce again and the couple would battle in the court system for three more years. She would file suit against Delany for failure to pay child support and in August of 1976 she won a contempt citation against him. In March of 1977, both consented to drop the legal battle and in July 17 of 1977 Genene's second child, Heather, was born. She later admitted that Heather had been conceived out of wedlock when she and Delany had another brief coming to terms.

Genene would then move back in with her adopted mother who helped with the babies as she began her training at San Antonio Independent School District's School of Vocational Nursing. Genene was a mediocre high school student but she excelled in the program, earning high grades. She aced the licensing exam and got a job at Methodist Hospital.

Genene only lasted eight months, however, getting fired when she made decisions about patient care in which she had no authority as well as being rude to patients. Genene would later claim that she was fired for standing up to a doctor who was being rude to a patient.

"She was a compulsive liar when she was a kid," Foster said. "And the lying continued into her adult life as it turned into full blown denial. She was never at fault for anything. It was always someone else, doctors, nurses, her mother, her husband. She never lived in the land of responsibility."

REIGN OF TERROR BEGINS

Genene then found work at Bexar County Hospital (now known as the University Hospital of San Antonio) where she was assigned to the Pediatric ICU.

It is here where the trouble officially began.

Her first patient had a fatal stomach disease called necrotizing enterocolitis and the boy died after surgery. Genene did not handle it well, crying hysterically. "She just went berserk," Cherylyn Pendergraft said, the RN that was orienting Genene during this time. Genene went so far as to move a stool toward the baby's cubicle and just sat there staring at the body.

Pendergraft felt the gesture odd considering that Genene had barely cared for the child.

Nonetheless, Genene saw herself as an equal to the RN's on duty and worked extra hard to acquire more knowledge than an ordinary LVN.

She worked the graveyard shift upon hire then transferred to the swing shift where she worked f3 p.m to 11 p.m while frequently volunteering for overtime and extra shifts.

Genene soon took on a reputation as the "nurse who cried wolf" to the many resident doctors who were training at the hospital. She would issue warnings about a child's worsening condition to the intern. If the intern did nothing she would then go to the resident doctor. If that physician did nothing then she would go higher up the chain of command and wouldn't stop until her recommendations were addressed.

Despite her eagerness to be perceived as on the same level as a registered nurse, Genene would skip continuation classes on the proper use of pharmaceuticals. In her first year, she was written up on eight separate occasions for giving the wrong dosage.

Genene wouldn't let any reprimands stop her, however, as she soon became the ward bully in the cramped quarters of the pediatric ICU. She would intimidate other nurses with her coarse demeanor, making more than a few transfer out of the unit to get away from her.

Her bullying tactics enabled her to make the unit her own, as she was the foul-mouthed Queen of the ward, bragging about her sexual escapades and making inappropriate remarks.

"Here we see the beginnings of tacit approval," Foster said. "No one at the hospital wants to put themselves on the line to stand up against her. It is an environment where everyone is trying to cover their own ass. No one wants to play snitch even when this woman is saying and doing all of these inappropriate things."

Even more disturbing is that Genene would also predict which baby would die.

During "report", a time in which the nurses would describe the conditions of their patients during the shift change handover to the next nurse, Genene would play the role of the Grim Reaper.

"This patient is really bad," she'd say forewarning the nurse, or even predicting death."This patient isn't going to make it."

By 1981, Genene would always demand to be assigned to the sickest patients. She seemed to enjoy the adrenaline rush of the code blues and would grieve when the child expired. Genene would hold the dead bodies and sing to it, making sure she would be the one to take the corpse to the morgue.

"She had a twisted hero complex," Foster said. "She thought of herself as equal to any RN. Most LVNs defer to the registered nurses out of education and experience. But it was quite the opposite with Genene. When the shit hit the fan she would be the first to come to the rescue. The problem was that she created these situations where she could be seen as the hero. Remember she didn't give them enough medication to kill them outright. She gave the babies just enough of a dose so that they would go into cardiac arrest. She wanted to be seen as the savior to the parents of the children she was killing. She wanted to be seen as the hero of the ward. This need was so deep-seated that she was willing to kill to get that need met. That need to be seen as a hero. That need to be seen as the most compassionate of all."

TOO MANY PATIENTS DYING

Co-workers became concerned that a surprising number of patients under the care of Jones were dying.

"The other nurses became concerned," said Vincent J.M. Dimaio, the chief medical examiner at the time. "That there were increased numbers of cardiopulmonary arrests on the ward. All her victims were children. The most innocent of the population. This would not have happened if the cases had been reported to the medical examiner's office."

Unlike most hospitals, Bexar County didn't lock their medications in a cabinet. When it become apparent that children were dying in the unit from non-fatal illnesses, the hospital dragged its feet in an investigation. There was a two-week period where seven children died in the unit. These deaths occurred only when Genene Jones was on duty and the patients were under her care.

"Astonishing," Foster said. "The tacit approval now extended to the cover up of children being murdered. The hospital administrators put their own public relations and jobs above the lives of children. It is a travesty of justice that no one at the hospital was ever punished for this."

Genene had an ally in the department in the form of Dr. James Robotham, however. Known as "JR", a reference to the ruthless businessman from the TV show Dallas, Robotham was an aggressive doctor throughout his tenure in the ICU. He had no problem dressing down nurses or student doctors who were not up to snuff or did not bend to his will. He had no hiring authority in the hospital but took on a vital role throughout the ICU by placing the patient's care onto his shoulders.

Genene saw a kindred spirit in Robotham and the doctor took a liking to her. There was one occasion in which he needed assistance and chose Genene over another nurse.

"She had been validated," Foster said. "She also wanted to be acknowledged for her nursing talents and finally there was someone who came along and anointed her as someone who was worthy."

"Robotham's Pet" as some of the nurses would later call her, would nonetheless display a macabre interest when a child came in with a fatal illness. Genene would make it clear that she wanted to be on hand when death inevitably came.

Genene would enjoy calling the parents to inform them of their child's death, sharing in their grief over the phone.

"She was Jekyll and Hyde," Foster said. "With the nurses and staff she would be coarse, demanding and condescending. But with the parents of the children she turned into the ultimate caregiver. Soft-spoken, compassionate, and joining them in their pain. She would have the parents believing that she was the most caring person on the face of the earth."

Never mind the fact that she would orchestrate the medical emergency of the child.

"That was her way of getting attention," Dimaio said. "She was a 'big person'. She was a 'big person' when she resuscitated children. When she brought them back from death's door. And the rest of her life, she wasn't anything."

THE KILLINGS MOUNT

A six month old baby named Jose Antonio Flores came into the unit with non-fatal symptoms: fever, vomiting and diarrhea. Unfortunately, he came under the care of Genene.

The baby soon suffered a seizure went into cardiac arrest and died.

Genene grabbed the dead baby and ran out of the department with the staff having to track down the crying LVN. The infant was later blood-tested and the results revealed that there had been an overdose of heparin, an anti-coagulant.

No one had ordered that the drug be administered and now the staff became suspicious.

When questioned about the baby's death, Genene resorted to manipulation and blackmail. She told the staff that she took records on every child that had died there and she knew which doctor had killed them.

Finally, one of the doctors informed the hospital administration what he suspected of Genene Jones. He had found a book in her possession about how to inject heparin through the skin without leaving a mark.

The hospital administrators, however, did not want the bad public relations fall out that would result from being a hospital that had a reputation for infant deaths.

"Say that they expected one (death) a week," Dimaio said. "All of a sudden they were getting three or four or five a week. I don't think there was any doubt that they had a good idea of what she (Genene) was doing."

"The amazing thing here is that even after the incident with the Flores' baby, Genene was allowed to continue working on the ward," Foster said.

Another child came into Genene's unit, this time to recover from open heart surgery. The child made progress but during Genene's shift he died.

"They notice that all of them (the deaths) were on the same shift," Dimaio said. "And all of them involved patients being taken care of by Genene Jones."

More doctors complained and a committee was set up to investigate. Head nurse Pat Belko and James Robotham were in charge on the hospital end but an outside team of investigators came in to look at the problem.

This third party team declined to put the blame on Genene as their findings were inconclusive.

COVERING THEIR ASS

Confident of they were in the clear, the hospital reports no abnormal deaths to the county medical examiner. Still, the hospital knew that Genene Jones was responsible for the deaths.

"She was left on the ward even though they knew what was going on," Dimaio said. "Someone said why don't we just fire her? Then they said well she'll just sue us and they'll be a big scandal. There were more interested in saving their reputation and not being sued then in the life and health of these children."

In order to avoid a public relations debacle, the administration decided to replace the LVNs in the unit with registered nurses. They said they were raising the "training bar" for ICU nurses and that LVNs would no longer be needed.

"So when they adopted that policy they let her go from that unit," Dimaio said. "Let go by the way, with an excellent letter of recommendation. Even though they knew what was going on."

Genene had been suspected in the deaths of over 47 other children, the NYT noted that the administration of Bexar County Medical Center and the University of Texas Medical school had shredded over 9,000 pounds of pharmaceutical records, records that were created during the time when Jones worked there.

By doing this, these administrators effectively destroyed any evidence that would be helpful in convicting Genene Jones of more crimes. The hospital stated that the shredding of documents was "routine" and a "coincidence", but the district attorney was able to intervene when, acting on a tip from an informant, he stopped the hospital from destroying an additional 50,000 pounds of pharmaceutical and medical records. The dean of medicine at Bexar was then cited for contempt of court when it was discovered that she withheld hospital reports from the grand jury.

"This is certainly an indictment of the hospital," Foster said. "If over 47 children were murdered, than there would have to be justice. The irony here is that the hospital administrators are not that far off from Genene Jones' mindset. They lie, deny and keep things in secret. All for the sake of control. All for the sake of being perceived that they are something they are not. Genene wanted to be seen as a hero but was really a killer. The hospital wants good pr at all costs, even childcare's lives. They are scum."

THE MURDERS CONTINUE

After her release from the county hospital and with a letter of recommendation in hand, Jones found work at a pediatric physician's clinic in Kerrville, Texas.

"She ended up here in Kerrville after she left San Antonio because of all these unexplained deaths," district attorney Ron Sutton said. "Genene Jones absolutely despises me because I brought down her little self-constructed impact."

The clinic was a start-up to be run by Dr. Kathleen Holland. She only had budget for an LVN and immediately thought of Genene Jones. She had remembered Genene and had been impressed by her take-charge personality and competence.

Holland contacted the human resource office at the hospital and inquired about the availability of Genene. Holland knew about the strange rumors about Genene but was willing to overlook them as she needed someone who could bring passion to their start up.

Holland didn't know how true those weird rumors were..

"She would create these medical emergencies," District Attorney Ron Sutton said. "That only she would know to handle. Then she would look like this supreme nurse when she would take care of the emergencies that she created."

Holland's revelation began with Petti McClellan brought in her young daughter Chelsea. McClellan said that Chelsea had a "bad cold" and went into the exam room with Dr. Holland. Genene then took the young baby out of Chelsea's arms, stating that she was going to "play" with the baby so that she and the doctor could talk.

"She had an irresistible compulsion," Foster said. "Doesn't matter where she is at, a hospital, a clinic, she has that compulsion. She'll see the opportunity to be a create the scenario for herself and she takes it."

"The protocol for the doctor's office would be the nurse, Genene Jones, would take the baby into a separate room just she and the baby, to perform whatever cursory examination; weight, blood pressure, whatever," Sutton said. "But during the time Genene would have these children by themselves all of a sudden they would become like a rag doll. And then she would scream out 'the baby's not breathing.'"

Moments later, Genene would cry out for help, saying that the baby couldn't breathe.

Doctor Holland immediately jumped into action, seeing that the baby had gone into a seizure. The child would be transported to a hospital and her life was spared.

The McClellan's expressed their gratitude toward Holland and Genene. They thought the world of the duo, believing that they saved the life of their child.

Little did they know that Genene had injected the child with succinylcholine.

Genene had used various methods to kill children under her care. She used injections of digoxin, heparin and later succinylcholine to cause a "code blue" in her patients. She would revive them afterward and receive praise. The succinylcholine she used is a paralytic that causes a temporary paralysis of skeleton muscles which can affect a patient's breathing. When she injected small children with this drug, the victim would suffer from cardiac arrest.

Petti would later return to the clinic months later with Chelsea. She had actually called the clinic to make an appointment for her son Cameron but Holland insisted that she bring Chelsea in so that she could "check on her."

"My daughter wasn't sick," Petti would later say.

Holland later disputes the claim that she asked Petti to bring Chelsea in instead of Cameron.

Unfortunately, Petti would bring Chelsea in and witness Genene administer two shots. The second shot would cause Chelsea to go into a seizure and later die.

"Once she began doing it," Foster said. "She couldn't stop. She became fueled by the adrenaline. The rush she got by sticking the syringe into the baby. The rush she got in waiting for the child to go into cardiac arrest. The the rush she got by watching the child die and comforting it in its death. She even got off on informing the parents of the baby's death. That is how twisted her mind was."

"Her original intent may not have been to kill," Foster said. "She was all about being seen as the hero, the Superwoman who came into save the day. Why she would target the same child coming in for another routine check-up really shows that she was getting careless about her victims. She had gotten away with it for so long that she didn't care. Plus, the compulsion would override whatever logic and forward thinking she had."

Chelsea's death was initially seen as sudden infant death syndrome.

"That's when we talked to the anesthesiologist," Sutton said. "He said that this child looks like it was coming out from the effects of succinylcholine, and we launched our investigation at that point."

"Soon as she got that first shot," Petti McClellan said, "Chelsey immediately starting reacting to it. And I asked her right off the bat, 'what did you do? What did you do? Something's wrong with her.'".

Genene visited Chelsey's grave and seemed genuinely remorseful.

"She was a psychopath with conflicted emotions," Foster said. "On one hand she had this need to kill and be in control of what others thought of her, specifically as a hero. And the other hand, she may have felt remorse when her 'heroic' efforts didn't produce the results she wanted."

Chelsey's mother, Petti, however, was shocked to see Genene at her daughter's grave.

Holland would later find puncture marks in a bottle of succinylcholine in a storage cabinet that only she and Genene had access to. "There were two holes in the lid of this bottle," Sutton said. "One where she had withdrawn and then she attempted to replace it with saline solution."

With the investigators closing in, Genene began to panic. She arrived at the clinic after lunch and complained to Holland that she was feeling ill...She had overdosed on her anti-depressants and began looking lethargic.

Holland immediately called the paramedics and Genene's stomach was pumped. Later upon her release, Texas Ranger Joe Davis interrogated her about the holes in the bottle of succinylcholine. Genene denied involvement, stating that she would be willing take a polygraph test.

The next day, Holland was shocked to see Genene report for work as if nothing had happened. She then informed Genene that her services would no longer be needed. Genene grew enraged and challenged Holland to take a polygraph. She then stormed out of the office.

Genene would later call back to the office and informed Holland's secretary that she had left a letter for the physician in her drawer.

The letter was a one page suicide note that she had written before she had taken the overdose of anti-depressants.

"There isn't anyway to explain to you why things are going to change. Sometimes, as wrong as it may seem, you have to except what life dishes out.

When your older, and I know your tired of hearing that, but you will be able to understand why, why I have to go away. It doesn't mean I don't love you. Please believe that. No amount of money or worldly goods could every buy my love. It is so deep & strong, it will last for all eternity.

Please explain if you can to Heather & Michael how much I love them. It's such a strong love, I can't put it on paper. I know I'm asking a lot, but I really feel your the only one who could do it.

I'm not guilty of murder, & I hope you believe that. But Daddy's way is right. It takes all the pressure off you and the seven people whose life I have altered.

No one can hurt me with my Daddy. He'll straighten this whole thing out & then we'll go home & everything will be alright. No more problems for you, no more nightmares for me.

Please make sure Michael and Heather are not separated. I know how my mother feels about Heather, but I also know how she feels about Michael. If Debbie or you can't take them together, please be sure whoever does are good people. People with lots of love.

Please don't be angry. I'm going with Daddy because I miss him and I want to be with him. He'll take care of both of us.

You'll be fine. Please believe that.

I love you,

Genene

Genene had attempted to frame Holland for the murders but all evidence pointed to her. All said and done, Genene had poisoned at least six children at the clinic. Three of the parents continued to utilize Holland as their pediatrician while three other families sued both Holland and Genene Jones as they believed that Holland knew or should have known about Genene's murderous ways.

The criminal investigation began and Chelsea's body was exhumed, revealing traces of the succinylcholine.

Her exact numbers of victims remain unknown as hospital officials first "misplaced" then destroyed records of her activities to prevent lawsuits after Genene's first conviction.

Genene would go on trial on January 15th, 1984 for the murder of Chelsea and injury to the other children. On February, 15, 1984, Genene was convicted of murder after a three hour deliberation. She was given the maximum sentence of ninety-nine years. In October, she went on trail for injuring Rolando Jones with an injection of heparin. She was sentenced a total of 159 years with the possibility of parole that came up after serving ten years.

In 1985, Gene was sentenced to 99 years in prison for killing fifteen month old Chelsea McClellan.

Later that year, she was sentenced to a term of sixty years in prison for the attempted murder of Rolando Jones with heparin.

"I've had several cases that stand out in my mind," Sutton said. "But this one is particularly heinous because of death to small children.

SERIAL KILLER TO BE RELEASED

Genene Jones is now set to go free because of a legal loophole in the form of She is now scheduled for mandatory release in February 2018 due to a Texas law that prevents prison overcrowding. Genene has been a prisoner who has exhibited "good behavior", becoming eligible for the release.

"Please, please, please, do not let this person walk," Petti McClellan said.

"Genene Jones is probably one of the worst types of serial killers because keep in mind who her victims were," said Andy Kahan, a victim advocate. "Defenseless, voiceless, babies. One of the nation's most diabolical serial killers in our country's history is set to be legally released,"

"I was so angry that it went on for so long," Cherlyn Pendergraft said. "That so many children had to die."

Jones now claims to be sickly and is housed in medical jail unit.

"Am I prepared that she walks?" McClellan asked. "No. Because she's gonna hurt another child. I don't want to hear that she's sick. Or that she's old, she's two years older than I am."

"There is absolutely no reason for Genene Jones to be walking the streets," Foster said. "She has a compulsion that has to be satiated. She needs to be locked up for the rest of her life."

The current District Attorney is looking to re-open old cases against Jones in order to keep her in prison.

KIMBERLY SAENZ

JAMIE PARKS

Kimberly Clark Saenz was a nurse. Almost ten years ago now, in 2008, she worked in a clinic called the DaVita Lufkin Dialysis Center. The clinic was- and still is- in Lufkin, a small blue collar city in East Texas of around 33,000 souls. But rather than care for her patients, she decided to kill. Because of a home life fraught with difficulties- she and her husband has fought, he had filed for divorce, and even taken out a restraining order against her- Kimberly's unrestrained and misdirected anger was taken out on her patients. And this was just the latest in a long list of healthcare jobs that Kimberly had held, after a spate of firings for various misdemeanours.

Even though she worked in a dialysis center, where there is normally little to cause complications and death, the number of patients dying on her watch alerted and disturbed other hospital staff. Even so, it took far too long for her managers and the authorities to find out what she had been doing. When, to their horror, they uncovered her crimes, Kimberly became national news.

Who was Kimberly Clark Saenz?

Kimberly hadn't had the best start in life. She was born Kimberly Clark Fowler in Fall River, Massachusetts in 1973. After an uneventful childhood during which she moved away from Massachusetts to Texas, she dropped out of high school in her senior year after falling pregnant. Kimberly and her husband would go on to have two children together, but Kimberly struggled with addiction and the strains this put on her home life.

She suffered from substance abuse problems, which proved to be a drain on the family finances; it was also enough to convince her to steal, which she did time and time again from her various employers. According to witness testimony at her trial, Lufkin law enforcement told the court that she had been arrested multiple times for intoxication and criminal trespass after domestic disturbances with her husband, Kevin Mark Saenz. She was clearly unhappy with the direction in which her life was heading.

Before taking the nursing position that would prove to be her last, Kimberly had been fired from four similar jobs in the recent past. Each time had been because she was caught stealing medication in her handbag once her shift was over. What is worse is that she lied each time to her prospective employer, claiming that she had no criminal history to speak of, even though when she applied for her final care work position she had actually been on bail. In this way it would be fair to say that the deaths Kimberly caused were as much as anything because of a failure of oversight, and a failure to correctly check employees' criminal histories.

But in the end, it took a letter from a top fire official to actually get the matter investigated. The letter was sent anonymously, but complained of the highly unusual number of patients being transferred to hospital. The letter was sent in April 2008, and read 'In the last two weeks, we have transported 16 patients. This seems a little abnormal and disturbing to my med crews. Could these calls be investigated by you?'

Surveyors arrived within the next few days to try and get a handle on the situation. But if anything, this blew the case wide open: they realised that over the course of the preceding month, emergency crews had been called out a total of thirty times, seven of whom had cardiac problems, and four of whom died. To anybody unaware of the normal operation of a dialysis center, this may or may not have seemed excessive; but in comparison to the previous fifteen months before then, emergency services had only been required twice, according to the Texas Department of Health Services. Because of the strict quality controls involved in green lighting medical equipment and medicine for public use, all signs pointed to another cause: a person.

How was Kimberly caught?

Kimberly was eventually caught out because of her own brazen attitude to the crimes she committed. More of the details would come out once the case was brought to trial, but a number of eye witnesses had separately and independently told Kimberly's superiors that they had seen her poisoning the people she was supposed to care for. On the morning of April 28th, Kimberly arrived at work at 4:30am, only to be told that she was no longer on the rota to work as patient care technician- in charge of medication- she was to work as a simple patient monitor, who would check up on patients over the course of the day, and perform basic cleaning duties. According to her supervisor Amy Clinton, Kimberly's response was strange: she began crying, wiping away tears, and said that that particular job was beneath her. Amy had only been working at the DaVita clinic for a few days, and had been called in because of two recent and unusual deaths.

At 6am, the two witnesses were brought to the clinic- Lurlene Hamilton and Linda Hall. They were suffering with failing kidneys, and dialysis was not unusual for either of them; indeed, patients often undergo the treatment at least three times a week, and the procedure can take hours. There's little to do but sit, read, or talk to family or other patients. They were around 40 feet away from another two patients named Marva Rhone and Carolyn Risinger. They watched as Kimberly Saenz poured bleach from a jug into a cleaning bucket, and then as she drew up a small amount of the bleach into a syringe. This first concerned the witnesses because they felt that whatever the bleach was being used for, the bucket was most likely an unsanitary place to draw it from.

But what shocked them was what happened next. Kimberly approached the two patients, Rhone and Risinger, and injected the bleach into the feed lines of the dialysis machines that they were hooked up to. Fortunately, neither went into cardiac arrest, presumably because Kimberly did not or could not inject enough bleach into the system. But the eyewitness testimony of Hamilton and Hall was proven correct during later analysis, which found bleach in Rhone's dialysis line. Bleach, of course, has a terrible effect on the body; it easily eats through tissue and when injected into the blood can cause blood cells to burst. Because of the overload of potassium this can cause in the blood stream, cardiac arrest often immediately ensues. That being said, bleach is generally eliminated from the body quite quickly, and if the victim survives, they very rarely suffer any further lasting effects.

A key point to understand is that bleach is regularly used in dialysis clinics across the country. First, of course, for general cleaning of the floors and walls: blood is easily spilled and contamination is a major risk. But in addition, bleach is the most common cleaning fluid used to clear dialysis lines after being used. As such, there are strict guidelines over its use: it should be clear that injecting it into the dialysis lines while still in use by patients is against those guidelines!

In addition to this eyewitness testimony, after just a brief analysis of the rota, one of the inspectors found that Kimberly had been working on a staggering 84% of the shifts when a patient suffered either chest pain or cardiac arrest. She had been working there in an entry level position for eight months up until that point, and this bizarre discrepancy was enough to get Kimberly fired in April 2008.

On the same night as those final attacks, Lufkin Police officer of thirteen years Bradley Baker was called out to Mark Kevin Saenz's home at around 8:30pm. The couple had split not long ago. Baker described what happened next during his testimony at trial: "Ms. Saenz was banging on the door of the house. Her eyes were glassy and she was having trouble answering questions." Baker issued a criminal trespass warrant to Kimberly, and upon talking to her further she admitted that she was taking Cymbalta and drinking. She was arrested for public intoxication, and at this point, the police knew nothing of what she had done earlier that day at the dialysis clinic.

Kimberly on trial

When Kimberly was brought to trial, she faced five separate murder charges over the deaths of Clara Strange, Thelma Metcalf, Garlin Kelley, Cora Bryant and Opal Few. She was accused of having killed them through poisoning them with sodium hypochlorite- better known to us as bleach- through injecting it into their dialysis lines. In fact, two eyewitnesses claimed that she had attacked two different patients on the date of April 28th, 2008. Her attorneys argued that she had been set up: she was a scapegoat for the DaVita clinic, which had been failing its patients long before the spate of deaths that April in 2008.

The two witnesses, Linda Hall and Leraline Hamilton, claimed that those two patients- Marva Rhone and Carolyn Risinger- had been injected with bleach that day. In addition, the Food and Drug Administration (FDA) prepared a report which confirmed that samples from a number of the victims had indeed tested positive for bleach, and while other samples were unclear, there was evidence that bleach "may have been present at one time." To come to that conclusion, they examined blood tubing, syringes and IV bags which had been used for the patients' dialysis.

The information about Saenz that came out during trial was shocking, and did nothing to dispel the idea that she should never have been allowed in a position of care. She had previously been fired from Woodland Heights hospital for stealing Demerol, which had been found in her handbag at the end of a shift. Very soon after having been fired from the DaVita clinic, she was suspended from the profession and her nursing licence was taken away. In between her firing and the trial, she worked as a receptionist without disclosing why she had been forced to find employment.

Kimberly refused to take the stand in her own defence, but her lawyers argued that she was a good woman who could never fathom killing another human being. 'Kimberly Saenz is a good nurse, a compassionate, a caring individual who assisted her patients and was well liked,' one of her defense attorneys, T. Ryan Deaton, told the court. And in a pre-recorded video message, Kimberly told the court that she felt 'railroaded' by the clinic; she had been the fall guy for the clinic, which desperately needed somebody to pin their failings on.

Her defense team argued that the marital issues and family strife she had been through prior to the murders had been overemphasised by the prosecution. To try and prove their point, they called upon an extensive number of character witnesses who each testified that Kimberly was not the woman she was made out to be in the press. If anything, she was a good woman, a caring woman who loved her family despite her struggles with addiction.

The first witness they called upon was Vernon Dean Warren, who had been dating Mark Saenz's mother at the time of the murders. He testified that he held no ill will against her at all, and that she was welcome to his home anytime. A friend of Kim's, Peggy Wells, also took to the stand to defend her friend. She had met Saenz in kindergarten, so had known her for well over thirty years. Peggy felt that Kimberly was no danger to either society or to her children.

Next up for the defence was Wendy Bryan, who had met Kimberly while she worked at Fleetwood Transportation, and where Kimberly had worked for several years. She told the packed courtroom that Kimberly had been a model employee, and that her personal troubles should not cloud anybody's mind about the person Kimberly really was. Asked about whether she felt that Kimberly was a good employee and a good person despite her personal issues, Wendy responded: "I would have absolutely hired her. Absolutely, without a doubt."

Another former employee of Fleetwood Transportation, Tonya Monlar, testified that Kimberly was "a very hard worker, very thorough." She even said that no matter what the outcome of the trial turned out to be, she would still keep in touch with Kimberly because she believed her to be a genuine and good person. "If I can visit, I'll visit. I'll write, and she's always in my prayers," she told the court. Yet another character witness was Barbara Allen, who had taught both Kim Saenz and her son. She told the court that Kimberly was a caring mother who had sacrificed her own schooling to go through with having her firstborn despite being so young. The local elementary school principal described how Kim was dedicated to her son: "When [he] was younger, he played baseball with my son. Kim was always there," said Karen Schumaker. And she described Kim's daughter as "a great kid".

Kimberly had sworn in an affidavit that she had no criminal record whatsoever, but a basic check revealed her extensive list of felonies: including the overuse and misuse of prescription drugs, general substance abuse problems, theft and violence. Prosecutors branded her defence a joke, calling it 'absolutely ridiculous'. They painted her as both a depressed and disgruntled employee, who on the testimony of her fellow nurses was always complaining about her patients, in particular those who required extensive care. They had even found evidence from her computer that she had searched for information on the Internet about bleach poisoning, whether bleach could poison a person through being injected into the blood, and whether bleach was traceable.

At one point in the trial, the victims of Kimberly's crimes were encouraged to speak and testify as to the misery she had caused. Thelma Metcalf's daughter told Kimberly: "You are nothing more than a psychopathic serial killer. I hope you burn in hell". The prosecution were also completely straightforward in their assessment of Kimberly's role and her obvious guilt: "The only days there were deaths in April, she was there," the attorney for the prosecution said. "Dialysis patients are sick, but every source of information we can find says it is very unusual for patients to die during dialysis treatment."

The attorney for the prosecution was Clyde Herrington. He believed that there were far more victims than those which were being discussed at the trial, an opinion based on the research of an epidemiologist at the Center for Disease Control and Prevention. That research categorically connected Saenz to the crimes, so it was a shame that Lufkin Police detectives were only able to find evidence from the two weeks prior to Kimberly being sacked. As such, there was nowhere near enough evidence to bring a successful case for those other victims; although given Kimberly's obvious guilt, and her modus operandi, it was plain to see that she had done far more damage than the few victims she was on trial for.

Kimberly's defense knew that she stood little chance of being found innocent of the charge of murder. So, rather than argue for her to be set free, they tried to have her charge of capital murder reduced to one of first degree murder- in other words, she would be in prison for life no matter what, but could avoid the death penalty. In summary, another of Kimberly's defense attorneys named Steve Taylor told the jury "She's never getting out no matter what you do... Society is protected. You will never see her again." Taylor also pointed out to the jury that Kimberly had been free during the period of the trial, and that prosecutors could not demonstrate that she had been a danger to the public.

To prove their point, the defense brought in Frank G. AuBuchon, a retired former employee of the Texas Department of Criminal Justice. Through him, the defense wanted to prove that just because they were pushing for something other than the death sentence, that Kimberly could never be a danger to the community again. Describing Kimberly's probable sentence, AuBuchon said: "It's a true life sentence. These people will die in custody." On the topic of what her life behind bars would be like, he said "You very quickly in prison the easiest way to do your time is to behave yourself. You get more privileges... Mind your own business. Don't tell anybody why you're there. Obey the rules." Finally, Frank Taylor told the court: "You will never see them again in society. They belong in another society now, the prison society."

On the other hand, during their summation, the prosecution did not specifically push for the death penalty. But they did remind the jury of Kimberly's criminal past, her issues with prescription drugs, and her propensity to lie to get what she wants. Just before the jurors retired to consider their verdict, Clyde Herrington told them: "I know you'll reach a verdict that's just and in accordance with the law," while showing them photos of the many victims who had suffered and died because of Kimberly and her actions. It was the prosecution that got what they wanted.

Kimberly was found guilty on March 31st, 2012, on the charge of capital murder, which covered each of the five murders. It was also clear that she had attacked, injured and killed far more patients than just those five. Just a few days afterwards, on April 2nd 2012, the jury sentenced Kimberly on behalf of Angelina County to life in prison with no hope of parole, and three separate twenty year sentences for aggravated assault. She remains in prison to this day.

What made Kimberly kill?

For anybody with even a passing knowledge of true crime, 'nurses who kill' are a recognisable and uniquely interesting subgroup of serial killers who continue to fascinate the American public. Genene Jones killed anywhere between six and sixty infants as a pediatric nurse in the '70s; Kristen Gilbert, 'the Angel of Death' killed four and tried to kill two more with epinephrine as a nurse in Massachusetts. Judy Buenoano, another nurse, was sentenced to die by electric chair for killing a string of previous husbands.

This isn't to suggest that there's something horrible about nurses! But the same trope is seen across the globe. Take Britain's Harold Shipman for instance: one of the UK's most infamous serial killers was a doctor, not a nurse, but killed at least 250 people over the course of decades. Each of these cases is tied to the others by the unique horror of killers who were supposed to care; murderers who were supposed to cure.

They are also linked by the fact that the underlying cause of all this misery and death is often inexplicable. Harold Shipman, for example, never expressed guilt or remorse. He maintained his innocence until his suicide in prison, as did his wife Primrose. As part of their case against Kimberly, the prosecution didn't actually have to prove her motive. But Clyde Herrington did speak to a registered nurse, one who had done extensive research into nurses and doctors who kill. But her research-which took in over a hundred killers- couldn't point to any unifying motive.

As Herrington put it to the jury, "Criminal behavior is something we've been trying to understand since Cain killed Abel. Only when the health care killer confesses do we know motive." But what Herrington claimed was that Kimberly had been driven to kill by her own troubles with both prescription drugs and her failing marriage. "From talking to some of the folks who worked with her, it sounded like her husband didn't want her to quit (DaVita)," Herrington continued. "She was depressed. She was frustrated, and I think she took those frustrations out on the patients."

How did Kimberly get away with her crimes for so long?

Kimberly Saenz's defense attorney, Ryan Deaton, claimed that the DaVita clinic was already plagued by malpractice and unusual deaths long before Kimberly started working there. Prior to the beginning of the trial, Deaton had fought hard for the jury to be able to see a report by the U.S. Department of Health and Human Services, which had been heavily critical of the DaVita clinic and its working practices. It had been ruled inadmissible by the state District Judge, Barry Bryan.

The report supposedly claimed that from December 1st 2007 until April 28th 2008, the clinic had overseen nineteen deaths, while over the entirety of 2007 there had been 25. Overall, this put the clinic above the state average, but only by seven percent.

But more importantly, the DaVita clinic was also accused within this report of shoddy record keeping that put patients at risk. Over the period between September 1st 2007 and April 26th 2008, 102 patients from the DaVita clinic had been transported to a local hospital either during or immediately after their dialysis treatment. Of these 102 patients, 68 cases had not been fully written up with a complete adverse occurrence report. So even though it was undoubtedly Kimberly who killed those people- there was no other way for bleach to make its way into the dialysis machines, and she was seen by two separate eyewitnesses with the syringe filled with bleach in her hand- the shoddy record keeping allowed an environment in which somebody who wanted to do what Kimberly did could get away with it.

The report summarised its findings with a damaging conclusion on the DaVita clinic and the ability of its staff. Their findings suggested that the DaVita clinic and its staff "did not demonstrate competence in monitoring patients during treatment alerting nurses or physicians of changes to a patient's condition and following the physician's orders for the dialysis treatment." In response a spokesman for the DaVita clinic, Vince Hancock, said that the company's actions did not lead to any deaths in April 2008, and that the court case proved it. "We hope that healing can start to occur for families of victims and for our teammates who also have been victimized by the murderous acts of Kim Saenz," he told the press.

Kimberly's retrial

Unbelievably, Kimberly and her defense lawyers felt that she stood a chance of winning an appeal, and they immediately sought leave to fight their case in the Court of Appeals. But the judgment of her first trial was upheld in a decision issued in August 2015. "Although both the jury charge and argument of counsel weigh in favor of egregious harm, we conclude the state of the evidence and the record as a whole substantially support a finding of guilt in regard to each of the capital murder victims," the opinion stated. "Accordingly, we hold the record does not establish egregious harm, and we affirm the trial courts judgment."

One of the central points of the appeal was that the Angelina County district court had allowed the jury to find her guilty, even though they could not unanimously agree on which exact patients had been killed by Kimberly; the judge had felt it to be obvious enough that she had killed at least some of the patients who had died, due to circumstantial evidence and eyewitness accounts.

The court dismissed each of the 21 issues which Saenz put before them, and had initially issued their ruling on January 22nd, 2014, but this ruling was itself overruled in December of that same year by the Texas Court of Criminal Appeals. The appeal was then sent back to the Fourth Court of Appeals, but she was again unsuccessful. Herrington, the original attorney for the prosecution, claimed that she would have appealed no matter what the grounds, but he didn't think she would be very successful. "Kim Saenz is sentenced to a life without parole," Herrington said. "She has absolutely no reason to continue to appeal as long as the possibility even exists."

Kimberly remains in prison to this day, universally considered guilty of the crimes she was sentenced to. She has no chance of parole; the only downside is that we may never know exactly what motivated her to kill.

KILLER NURSE BEVERLY ALLITT

JENNIFER PARRIS

Beverly Allitt-the Angel of Death

It is hard to believe that a young female could be capable of murder, let alone multiple murders. It is even more shocking that a female nurse could carry out such terrible crimes. That is exactly what Beverly Allitt did though. This nurse is Britain's most infamous female serial killer and also goes by the name of the Angel of Death due to her responsibility to care for others but instead used her nursing position to kill people. Over a short period of fifty-nine days in her job as a nurse in a children's ward, she killed four young children and attempted to kill at least nine others either by causing cardiac arrest or hypoglycemia. The Angel of Death did not appear to be an evil killer though. She was very well mannered with parents, which is how she gained their trust with their precious loved ones. But after similar/suspicious causes of death in the children's ward, investigations at the hospital showed missing nursing records and the presence of Allitt with every one of those cases.

Childhood

As a child, Beverly Allitt liked attention and would go about negative ways of getting it. She was born in October of 1968 and was one of four children (two sisters and one brother). Her father worked in an off-licence (a British shop where the liquor is sold off premises) and her mother cleaned schools. Neighbors described Allitt as affectionate because she liked to volunteer and often would babysit. She did her chores at home and saved the money she earned. Teachers also really liked her and was considered one of their favorites. She went to school at Charles Read Secondary Modern School because she failed the exam needed to attend Kesteven and Grantham Girls' School.

She often would wear casts and bandages as a kid without letting her injuries be examined. She got worse as she got older and became overweight. During this time in her life, she was sick and injured more frequently. She often engaged in self-injury and spent a lot of time in and out of various hospitals due to different ailments such as gall bladder pain, back trouble, ulcers, headaches, and blurred vision, just to name a few. Her reasons were that she had been hit on her bike by a passing car or had fallen off a horse or even had been burned. Most of her problems were either made up or self-inflicted. She convinced a doctor to take out her healthy appendix. Then, she constantly interfered with the scar to keep it from healing. Another time, she stabbed herself in the hospital with the intention of injecting her body with water. Next, there was the time when she tampered with a thermometer in the hospital. Because she was physically healthy, she had to see lots of different doctors in order to keep them treating her.

Allitt was a frequent liar and not just about her illnesses. She would often make up stories. One time, she told people that her parents had split up and that she would have to go live with her aunt. The tales would be investigated and found out to not be true.

Beverly Allitt dreamed of becoming a nurse and attended school at Grantham College and began her studies at the age of sixteen. During her last year of school, she was absent approximately one hundred and twenty-six days with numerous illnesses. Nurses there also described her as odd. There were some at the school that thought Allitt would benefit from psychiatric help.

She did manage to find a boyfriend at Grantham College really only because she forced Stephen Biggs to be hers. He bought her a ring but she never set a date for the wedding and refused to hold his hand in public. Once, she faked a pregnancy. She said that Stephen had AIDS. Another time, she lied about being raped by a former boyfriend. Allitt was described as deceptive by her boyfriend.

Eventually, Allitt's odd injuries (real or fake) were thought to be from a controversial personality disorder known as Munchausen Syndrome. People with this disorder like to be ill because of the attention they get from others when they are sick as well as the satisfaction of fooling doctors with their self-inflicted illnesses and injuries. They often have long medical histories. They are frequent liars and have lab tests that lead to no answers for the doctors to diagnose a patient. Allitt may have liked the attention because even though her childhood seemed to be relatively normal, there could have been emotional needs that were not being met.

Nursing Career

Beverly Allitt went on to become a nurse but the odd behavior from her childhood still continued. She took her nursing exams and actually failed them because she was absent quite often due to her various illnesses.

After that, Allitt managed to find a job at a nursing home. Like at school, she was gone quite often. Once, when she was there, it was thought that she smeared feces on the walls.

In 1991, at the age of twenty-three, Beverly Allitt surprisingly got a six-month contract job at Grantham and Kesteven Hospital that is located in Lincolnshire working in the children's ward. This ward was for newborn babies up to the age of sixteen. Kids sent to this hospital often had minor illnesses. They were quickly treated and then sent home as soon as they were well.

When Allitt arrived at the hospital, she had had less than two years of experience at this point and was not even a qualified children's nurse. It was shocking that she even was considered for a job considering how many days of class she missed when attending nursing school. The only reason she got the job was because the hospital was understaffed and no one else applied for the job. At the time, there were only two day nurses and one night nurse. According to one of those nurses, Mary Reet, who worked at the hospital at the same time as Allitt, "There was something about her that I didn't like but couldn't pinpoint it" (Birmingham Mail). She thought that she seemed cheerful, friendly, and helpful, however. Allitt was even respected. She was the one calling the alarms and identifying problems that the very sick children were experiencing.

Because of her job working with others, it meant that she was no longer getting personal attention but it allowed her to find attention in other ways that were just as negative as when she was a kid. The nurse was able to use this opportunity to get close to the patients. Allitt was able to befriend all of her patients' parents by suggesting that they leave to go get some coffee. Through this recommendation, the parents were trusting her and allowing her to be alone to administer treatment to the children. The parents had really appreciated the nurse at the time because of her actions during this difficult time when their children were sick. It was her care and love for her patients that caused the parents to call her an angel. She would even ride with the patients in the ambulance if they needed to be transferred to another hospital. However, Allitt was far from an angel. The term Angel of Death is given to medical professionals that are supposed to be healing patients but are really causing them harm.

The angel changed a week after she arrived at the hospital and odd things began to happen. Money was being stolen from the nurses. A key to the insulin refrigerator had disappeared. This is also when the young patients began experiencing odd symptoms that were very serious. Some of the patients died. At Grantham and Kesteven Hospital, usually only one child died a year. Once Allitt started working, four children died in just a period of a few months.

The Victims

Allitt's reign of terror began on February 21, 1991. Though it is not exactly clear how many children she actually did harm, the definite numbers are four murders and nine that were purposely harmed all within a fifty-nine-day time period. The ages of her patients were between seventeen weeks to eleven years old.

Seven-month-old Liam Taylor was Beverly Allitt's first victim. He had a chest infection and had come to the hospital for treatment. Since Allitt was able to befriend the parents, they left the hospital to get some rest. Once they returned, they learned from her that Liam had experienced respiratory problems but had recovered. She tried to convince the parents to leave again but they chose to stay. He suffered more respiratory problems under Allitt. She let the emergency team at the hospital know once he started becoming pale. The other nurses on the floor were confused because no alarms sounded when he had stopped breathing. He did survive but he had suffered cardiac arrest and brain damage. He was put on life support and was later taken off of it by his parents. His death at the time was ruled as heart failure.

Timothy Hardwick was Allitt's next victim. He was the oldest victim at eleven. He had cerebral palsy and dealt with seizures. The emergency team was notified when the boy turned blue and had no pulse. Allitt stood by as the defibrillator was used. Unfortunately, the boy died. There was an autopsy performed but there were no answers to the cause of his death. Epilepsy was eventually ruled as the cause.

The third victim was one-year-old Kayley Desmond. She had a chest infection but was getting better. After being in the care of Allitt though, she went into cardiac arrest. She was revived and transferred to another hospital. Once there, doctors discovered that there was a puncture hole under her armpit and also an air bubble. It was decided that it was probably due to an accidental injection. Because Kayley was transferred to the other hospital, she did survive.

Allitt's next victim was five-month-old Paul Crampton. He had been admitted for a minor infection. The nurse was not actually on duty when he was admitted but after she took over, Paul's condition deteriorated. He experienced an episode of insulin shock and nearly went into a coma. The Angel of Death was the one that raised the alarm about his serious condition. Doctors were very confused about the changes in insulin levels. After a few days, Paul began to feel better and Allitt was asked by the doctor to remove his drip. Shortly after that, he became quite ill for the second time. When he started feeling better, the dad decided to take a short break from the hospital room. The nurse was once again left in charge and the baby suffered the third attack. He was transferred to another hospital. Allitt actually went with him in the ambulance. She was also the one that had suggested that the doctors test the baby's blood sugar. Thankfully, Paul survived at the other hospital. After a few weeks, his test results came back. He had actually had 43,147 milliunits of insulin in his blood. That is one of the highest levels found in a human. The only other person that had levels this high died. It was a wonder that Paul survived with Allitt as his nurse.

Next on Allitt's list was Bradley Gibson at five years old. He had pneumonia and under the care of the Angel of Death, went into cardiac arrest. It was discovered that he also had high insulin. That night, he had a heart attack but was transferred to a second hospital and was able to survive.

Yik Hung Chan was two when he came to the hospital to recover from a fractured skull from a fall. He ended up turning blue while Allitt was working. He was given oxygen, transferred to another hospital, and recovered. The nurse was not blamed though because it was thought that the fracture was behind the boy's symptoms.

Next, Beverly focused her attention on twins on two different occasions. The twins were born premature and were under her supervision. The first twin, Becky, was found to have been cold and hypoglycemic but was released that evening. Then, that night, Becky woke up in pain but a doctor just said it was colic. She died that night. That is why the second twin, Katie, came back to the hospital for observation. Katie stopped breathing a couple of times while there. Her lungs collapsed and she suffered from brain damage and was transferred to another hospital. There, it was also discovered that five of her ribs had been broken but surprisingly, she lived. Her parents were so happy that they asked Allitt to be Katie's godmother. She agreed despite Katie having to live with partial paralysis, sight and hearing damage, and cerebral palsy.

After this, there were four additional victims that also suffered from similar symptoms as the other patients over a short period of fifteen days. There was seven-year-old Michael Davidson, nine-month-old Christopher King, eight-month-old Christopher Peasgood, and seven-week-old Patrick Elstone. Patrick was oxygen deprived and became brain damaged. People were starting to get suspicious about what was going on at this hospital.

Finally, Claire Peck, age fifteen months, became Allitt's last victim. This little baby had asthma and required a breathing tube. She was only under the care of the nurse for a couple of minutes when she had a heart attack. She survived but then had a second one later, leading to her death. It was thought that her death was because of natural causes. It was later found that she had been injected with lignocaine. This drug is not administered to babies. Claire was the Angel of Death's last victim after fifty-nine days of work.

The Investigation

After the numerous number of cardiac cases in the last few months at Grantham and Kesteven Hospital, an inquiry was launched into the cause of all of them. Deaths and comas at children's hospitals are actually pretty rare; especially if they are unexplained. At this particular children's hospital, usually only one child died a year. At first, it was thought that maybe there was a virus in the air that was making the patients sicker than when they arrived. This turned out to be incorrect. The nurses on the floor, including Beverly Allitt, talked about how maybe there was a parent or some outsider sneaking in and causing harm. That was when security cameras were placed in the hospital and the staff became more careful. They were also being watched by other people that worked in the hospital.

Next, it was discovered that there was a lot of potassium in Claire's blood. The police were called into the investigation and realized that there was lignocaine in Claire's system. This drug is given to people during cardiac arrest but is never given to a baby.

It was then that the police began to suspect that all the deaths were probably not due to natural causes. In fact, there were a lot of victims that had had high levels of insulin. To figure out what was going on, the police had a secret meeting with the hospital management to talk about a possible killer. After that, information came about that Allitt had actually reported that the key to the refrigerator where the insulin was stored had gone missing.

The next thing to do was check the daily nursing logs. Coincidentally, they were missing. The pages for the time of Paul Crampton's visit had been torn out of the book. There was also another record book that was gone. The pages were actually discovered at Allitt's house. The missing records along with her presence at every incident involving the mysteriously ill children led to her arrest.

Mary Reet, one of Allitt's coworkers was actually stunned at first to hear of her arrest. She was sure that the police had made a mistake. In fact, Katie's parents wanted to protect their daughter's godmother. They hired a detective to help prove her innocence. They even let the nurse continue to babysit Katie. Other people in the United Kingdom were also shocked. There had never been a nurse that had killed patients in the country. But with the evidence that had been collected, there was definitely no mistake about who was guilty of harming thirteen or more innocent hospital patients that were all so very young.

The Arrest/Trial

The police thought that they had enough evidence to convict Allitt but she was not actually charged until several months later. When interrogated, she did not seem scared about talking to the police. She denied any wrongdoing and said that all she had been doing was caring for the ill children. She even claimed that she was not at the hospital on some of the days in question and that at the other times she had come on the scene later and that she had been trying to help like a good nurse would do. At that point, the police did not have enough evidence to convict her so they had to let her go for the time being but that still did not erase their suspicions and she was suspended from the hospital. After all, the events at the hospital were certainly suspicious. Also, the other nurses said that she never liked to pick up crying babies and that she never seemed saddened by the deaths of any of the children. Later, she was eventually arrested.

With the investigation of Allitt's Munchausen Syndrome that led her to desire attention through the suffering of various medical conditions, it was also found that she dealt with Munchausen Syndrome by Proxy. This personality disorder is very similar to Munchausen Syndrome but instead of making oneself ill, the individual makes another one ill in order to get attention. People with Munchausen Syndrome sometimes also have Munchausen Syndrome by Proxy like Allitt. In Beverly situation, when the nurse found that she was no longer getting attention for her own medical disorders, she switched to causing them because she was able to receive attention from parents and other nurses by acting like the hero for the victims when she cared for them. The victims of people with Munchausen Syndrome by Proxy are usually children because they are unable to speak up for themselves. Allitt was made out to look like a hero at times while still working at the hospital because she was caring for the children that had become seriously ill. She was even able to diagnose some of the children's ailments rather than the doctors since she had caused the illnesses. Such as in the case of Katie, the twin, Allitt was made godmother which gave her the attention she craved.

Despite her love of attention, she did not want the attention for being a criminal. She wanted what she thought was positive attention in which people pitied her since she was sick quite often.

Allitt was evaluated by medical professionals for her disorders while in jail but she never did confess to the crimes. While she was awaiting trial however, Allitt lost a ton of weight which developed into anorexia. This was just another example of the psychological problems she experienced. Because of all of her past (and now present) illnesses, she repeated her absenteeism from nursing school and only attended sixteen days of the two-month long trial.

The trial was difficult because even though the evidence pointed to her, there were no fingerprints or any eyewitnesses. Everything was circumstantial. It had taken nearly nine months to gather the evidence that had been presented in court. The police were definitely worried about what the jury would decide. The jury deliberated for six days before they made the big decision about the Angel of Death.

She was eventually charged with four counts of murder, eleven counts of attempted murder, as well as eleven counts of causing serious harm to her patients. The parents of the victims, including the police, were overjoyed with the verdict. Justice would be served for what she had done to their children. The nurse was then given thirteen life sentences in 1993 for the murder and attempted murder of the innocent children that became her victims. Munchausen Syndrome by Proxy had no impact on the judge's decision of the extremely severe sentence that was given to Allitt. This is actually the harshest punishment ever given to a female. The judge said that he recommended that she spend at least forty years in prison before parole would even be considered but it became thirty years. As the judge said when she was sentenced, "You have turned the hospital where you worked into a killing field" (Birmingham Mail).

Allitt will be 54 in 2022 when the thirty-year possible parole could even become a possibility. It will only happen though if she has become a reformed person and is no longer a danger to herself or to anyone else. It does not change that she is still a murderer, despite having the label of Munchausen Syndrome or Munchausen Syndrome by Proxy. Though it does not seem likely that she will be released, the parents of the victims say that no matter what, they will fight back if there ever comes a chance of her leaving the prison/hospital where she is serving her time.

Prison

Allitt was sent to Rampton Secure Hospital in Nottingham to serve her sentence under the Mental Health Act. This hospital is a facility that has high security to protect prisoners suffering from mental disorders. It is not a prison because the patients/prisoners are there to receive treatment. Chris Taylor, the father of Liam Taylor, was not pleased with her placement. He thought she should be sent to jail and that it would not matter whether she killed herself in prison or not. She was sent to the hospital by the judge because of her history of self-harm. Taylor, however, looks at it as a place to take a vacation because she has a TV and is allowed to talk to other people at the hospital to form relationships with them. There is a bar and the hospital throws discos. Occasionally, Allitt has even been allowed to go out shopping as long as she is with a guard. During an interview, the former nurse mentioned that she liked the place because of the freedom it gave her that she would not receive in jail. In order for prisoners like Beverly Allitt to enjoy the freedom while receiving treatment, it costs the taxpayers of the United Kingdom £2000 a week for each inmate to stay there.2000

Her problems with Munchausen Syndrome have not ended despite being at Rampton Secure Hospital in order to receive her treatment. Once she arrived, she ate glass, stabbed herself with paperclips, and poured boiling water on her hands. On the plus side, she did admit to three of the murders and to six of the attempted ones.

Beverley was a young nurse that should have had the desire to help young children and be an advocate and a voice for them in order to heal. Growing up, she craved attention and went about negative ways to get it. She would either purposely hurt herself or lie about being ill in order to get attention. Things did not get better as she got older. Instead, she took advantage of her position at the hospital where she worked as a children's nurse. She harmed and killed many children so that she could get attention for herself. Through her attention desiring ways, she killed four children and hurt at least eleven more in the fifty-nine days that she worked as a children's nurse. Parents trusted the woman that later would become known as the Angel of Death. She will no longer be able to hurt another patient or child anymore since she has been given thirteen life sentences and will unable to be eligible for parole for at least thirty years (and that is only if she is able to show that she is no longer a danger to society).

SERIAL KILLER NURSE

CHRIS HAMPTON

Niels Hoegel

"Apparently some of his colleagues already called him bad luck charm because very often he was already around when a patient needed to be resuscitated so they just thought...you know...just by chance...he's around and he helps assist junior doctors but from what I've heard people suspected, there were suspicions, there were rumours but nothing...no evidence...nothing concrete."

Uli Hesse, Journalist.[1]

An Inconspicuous Beginning

Not much is known about the private life of Niels Hoegel, the life he led before he was catapulted (or rather catapulted himself) into the spotlight. But Niels Hoegel appeared to be a caring, compassionate man who seemed destined to spend his life helping other people.

Hoegel was born in Wilhelmshaven on December 30th, 1976. German reporting rules have kept most of the details of his personal life away from the public eye, but what is known is that Hoegel's father was also a nurse, at the Willehad Hospital. [2] His mother was a paralegal, and his older sister was a dentist – to all intents and purposes the entire Hoegel family was dedicated to helping others. His parents separated when Niels was just 11 years of age – a situation which he found difficult to handle. His ambition had always been to be a firefighter – however, this was never going to come to fruition because Hoegel suffered from acrophobia or a fear of heights.[3]

He was educated at the IGS (comprehensive school) in Wilhelmshaven, where his friends and former teachers remember him as a 'normal' student, widely accepted and fairly popular. He is described as funny and helpful, although his teachers made a point of remarking that he was less than engaged in class. While at school it appeared that the young Niels Hoegel was more interested in football than his studies, something which was borne out by the fact that he never graduated. When asked to describe him as a student, one teacher remarked that "he was a fairly normal student".

Hoegel was apparently less than forthcoming with the girls and was not the type to have the confidence to approach them in the school yard.

However, what he lacked in romantic aptitude he more than made up for in his medical studies, showing a predilection for medicine, giving his father high hopes that his son would go on to become a doctor. Perhaps it was his failure to live up to his father's expectations which planted the 'God Complex' in his mind – the complex which would take the lives of many people in the following years.

Niels Hoegel, the Nurse

When he was 17, Hoegel began his nursing studies at St Willemad Hospital, where he discovered the joys of alcohol, drugs, and members of the opposite sex, a time he described as 'the best phase of his life.'[3] However, once again his former friends and fellow students remember him as just being 'nice'. There was nothing remarkable or notable about the young man – he was just 'normal'.[4]]

After graduation, Hoegel took up a position at the Oldenburg Clinic on June 15th, 1999. For the first few weeks Hoegel, like all new staff, was accompanied by a senior member of staff.[5] The clinic was known as an excellent hospital, in particular with regards to its heart surgery intensive care unit. However, Niels Hoegel found himself floundering slightly under the stressful atmosphere and pressured conditions which a heart surgery center naturally entails. So stressful was it, in fact, that Hoegel described his first cardiac surgery as a "traumatizing experience". The effect on Hoegel was quite profound – he began to drink heavily and developed depression and anxiety.[6]

Things soon started to go wrong at the exemplary Oldenburg hospital. As the death rate of patients began to rise, so did the rumours. Hoegel's fellow nurses noticed that this increase in deaths coincided with his arrival at the clinic, but despite the whisperings around the hospital, nothing was officially noted. Without any firm evidence, the hospital decided not to go to the police - they felt that they could not take 'gut feelings' and suspicions to the authorities.[7]

Suspicions grew, and in August 2001 a meeting of doctors and nurses from the clinic was held to discuss the situation, a meeting which Niels Hoegel himself attended. It was pointed out that, whenever Hoegel was on duty, the number of deaths and/or the need for resuscitation was higher. Hoegel, of course, denied the allegations and following the meeting he took three weeks off work, claiming sickness. It was noted that, during his absence, only two patients died – much less than the figure which had become the norm during Hoegel's shifts.[8]

Hoegel returned to work in mid-September after his leave of absence and began working on the night shift. Once again the number of unexplained deaths rose. Almost straight away five patients become inexplicably ill, needing to be resuscitated an overall total of ten times. All five patients died – three immediately, and the remaining two a short time later. It had now become blindingly obvious that Niels Hoegel was behind the deaths – 58% of deaths at the hospital occurred under his care.[9] In September 2002 he was given the option to either resign or move to a more 'mundane' position within the hospital. Hoegel resigned. On October 10th, 2002, the nursing director of the Oldenburg hospital gave Hoegel a glowing reference, despite her full knowledge of the suspicions surrounding his conduct while working at her hospital. In the reference, her claims included terms which suggested that Hoegel had been a valuable member of staff, stating that he had worked "prudently, conscientiously and independently...in a critical way and has acted correctly" and that he displayed "willingness to serve, and cooperative behavior". In conclusion, she stated that "he had completed the tasks assigned to him to the fullest satisfaction".[10]

That reference sealed the fate of many patients who would be unfortunate to find themselves under Niels Hoegel's care in the coming months and years.

Delmenhorst

In 2003 Niels Hoegel moved to Delmenhorst, and a year later, in 2004, he got married. That same year his wife gave birth to a little girl. The birth, by all accounts, was a difficult one, even life threatening for the baby and Hoegel was forced to stand by and watch, unable to do a thing to help.[11] Could this helplessness have acted as a trigger? It certainly seems possible, likely even, because, in the months which followed, many more lives would be lost at the hands of Niels Hoegel.

Home for Hoegel and his family was a quiet residential area called Ganderkesee, an unassuming area midway between the city and the countryside. It was a good place in which to raise a family – people weren't afraid to go out at night, and there were plenty of families with children living close by. The Hoegel residence was a small semi-detached house, with space for parking, and a garden in which Hoegel's daughter could play.

Life was typically suburban. Niels would talk to his neighbors over the garden fence, passing the time of day and exchanging pleasantries with them. When one of his neighbors was pregnant, Hoegel kept a watchful eye on her and helped to look after her.[12] It was comforting to know there was a nurse living close by, someone the neighbors could go to for help if needed.

But there was another side to Hoegel, one that sometimes showed its face to the neighbors. Whenever the subject of an accident, for instance, came up Hoegel would make sarcastic comments about the victims, in direct contrast to the caring, compassionate nurse most people thought he was.[13]

Family life overwhelmed Hoegel, and he threw himself into his work, even choosing to spend his free time working for the Red Cross Ambulance Service rather than spending his time at home with his wife and daughter. Life was spiralling out of control, and he began to drink and take drugs more heavily.[14]

Towards the end of 2002, Hoegel found himself a new position, this time at the intensive care unit at Delmenhorst hospital.[15]

"He seemed to have been pretty unassuming...blended in in a way but obviously he had also this other side...that he wanted to show off his skills, but in a way, he seemed to be pretty relaxed and just a colleague for most of them."]

Following a car accident, although uninjured Hoegel began to take medication for the panic attacks which began soon afterwards. His substance abuse didn't go unnoticed among his colleagues.

"Alcohol, his medication, and even more work. It seems he also defined himself a lot about his job and about his work...so maybe that was one of the reasons he needed this feeling of being a hero."[16]

Intensive care was the perfect environment for Niels Hoegel.

"Patients in intensive care are the sickest patients in the hospital so there is a higher death rate there than there would be from a normal ward. So a higher death rate would not necessarily spark suspicions unless it was out of keeping with previous years or other intensive care units."[17]

Hoegel found himself once again at the center of staff room suspicions. It was already well known that the nurse was a heavy drinker and was becoming more and more reliant on prescription medications, but his colleagues were also curious as to why this highly skilled nurse had left his previous position at Oldenburg.

But that wasn't all. His behaviour was arousing suspicion about his professional conduct within Delmenhorst itself. Hoegel always seemed to be present when there was a patient in need of resuscitation, and it became something of a standing joke that he was a bad luck charm – bringing death to his patients whenever he was on duty. But, just as was the case with Oldenburg, nothing was done about the suspicions.

Until Hoegel got careless.

"He was only caught by chance. We assume that he injected a patient on the intensive care unit...with the heart drug. And we know that a nurse came into the room just when the patient went into cardiac arrest, and somehow she was a little bit...something wasn't quite right, so she helped resuscitate the patient, and afterwards checked and she found five vials of this particular heart drug in one of the wastebaskets on the intensive care unit. She didn't know that he had just injected a patient who was stable with this particular heart drug and he fell into a cardiac arrest. The nurse realized that he needed to be resuscitated. She did this...a colleague helped her...but she was kind of suspicious. She found the entire situation very strange because the patient had been stable. So she talked with her colleague and her colleague found, also by chance, empty vials of this particular heart drug in a wastebasket on the intensive care unit. And that's how it all started."

The empty vials had contained a drug called Ajmalin, an antidysrhythmic drug which is used to slow down the heart rate of a patient whose heart is beating at an abnormally high rate. Hoegel's victims, however, had normal heart rates, so when they received the Ajmalin, their heart would slow to a dangerously low level, often resulting in cardiac arrest.

The suspicious nurse took her concerns to her colleagues.

The patient in question was in intensive care suffering from lung cancer and had no heart issues which would have necessitated the use of the drug.

Arrest

This time the suspicions were taken seriously, and Niels Hoegel was arrested and charged but incredibly he was allowed to continue working. With no prior suspicions against him (that they were aware of) the authorities believed it was a one off, a mistake perhaps, or a momentary lapse in judgement. The case was treated as one of negligence, rather than homicide.

The case went to trial, and in 2008 nurse Niels Hoegel was found guilty of one charge of manslaughter and was sentenced to seven and a half years.

And there it might have remained, had a woman who had been following the case not come forward.

"A woman heard about that story, and she went to the police because she suspected that her late mother was also killed by Niels, and that started a whole new investigation."[18]

Brigitte Arndt

On March 27th, 2003, Kathrin Lohmann waved goodbye to her 61-year-old mother, Brigitte Arndt, and left the Delmenhorst hospital to return home. It had been a worrying time for Kathrin – her mother had been seriously ill, but now the tide seemed to have turned and, having survived a coma, Brigitte was now on the mend and was looking forward to being discharged from hospital and going home with her daughter to her house in Berne.

But as Kathrin left the hospital she was overcome with a dreadful feeling of foreboding – a feeling that that would be the last time she saw her mother alive. She shook it off and went home.

Later on that evening, Kathrin called the hospital, as she did every night, to check on her mother's condition and to reassure herself that all was well. Something about the male's voice on the other end of the phone worried Kathrin, but nevertheless, she went to bed, safe in the knowledge that had there been anything of concern, the nurse would have told her.

But she was to hear that same male voice only a few hours later when the phone rang at 1.30 am, telling her that Brigitte's condition had deteriorated and that she needed to return to the hospital immediately.

Kathrin was met at the hospital by two doctors, who told her that, despite their best efforts, her mother had passed and that they had done all they could for her. Standing in the corridor, Kathrin cried and screamed for her mother.

Kathrin was filled with remorse. It had been at her own insistence that her mother had gone to the hospital in the first place – perhaps if she had not persuaded her to seek help she would still be alive. But her feelings of guilt slowly changed to doubt – doubt that her mother's death had been natural, doubt that the staff at the hospital had really done all they could for Brigitte. But there was nothing she could do – friends and family slowly drifted away, doubting her claims, and Kathrin's life went downhill. She slipped into a deep depression, and, unable to work she was forced to move into a one room apartment in a less than desirable area.

And that was her life, until five years later when she saw the story of Nurse Niels Hoegel's conviction for murder on the news.

She knew she had been right. She received no support from family and friends, who could not believe that she was going back over her mother's death again, but she was determined to get the truth about Brigitte, so she took her story to the police in Delmenhorst.

They looked into it, and found, to their interest, that Hoegel had been on duty in intensive care the night Brigitte had died. Kathrin pushed for answers and asked repeatedly for her mother's body to be exhumed. She came up against some strong opposition – the public prosecutor's office told her time and time again that exhumations were too expensive, but she persisted.

In spring 2009 Kathrin got her wish. Brigitte Arndt's grave, at Warfleth cemetery in Wesermarsch, was surrounded with covers as an excavator dug up her coffin, and her remains were taken away for examination. Once again, Kathrin was by herself, both emotionally and physically. There was no priest there to bless the body, and the grave was waterlogged from the nearby dyke. Kathrin wondered if she had disturbed her mother's body for nothing – she was afraid the water might have washed away what little evidence there might be.

She had a long wait, but finally, after many more calls to the prosecutor's office, Kathrin had her answer. Traces of Ajmalin, which is found in the drug Gilurytmal, was discovered in Brigitte's system. Niels Hoegel had murdered her mother.[19]

More Horror

Following Kathrin Lohmann's suspicions and the subsequent proof that Niels Hoegel had murdered her mother, police prepared for the mass exhumation of many more bodies.

When questioned about Brigitte's murder, Hoegel admitted his guilt.

"He made the police's life quite easy by admitting to having killed people in the past. Now, these kinds of killers don't just admit things because they feel remorse or because they're sorry for what they've done. He would have seen some benefit to him in admitting it. He probably recognized that the game was up and that it would be beneficial to him in terms of [a] shortened sentence or the amount of attention he might receive, to admit it."

Hoegel's admission was not as straightforward as it seemed. By causing his patients to crash, and then bringing them back, or attempting to bring them back, to life, Hoegel was always in the limelight, ever the hero. And his confession to the police about having killed more patients only served to keep the attention on him.

"Having admitted that he had killed people, he kind of threw down the gauntlet to the police. He'd made it easy in one way but made it very difficult in another way because he wouldn't give them any details and he was saying that he couldn't remember, and his story kept changing, which is a tactic often used by these kinds of people to keep the attention on themselves. So the police then had to go and get the hard evidence to be able to take him to court, and unfortunately, that meant exhuming a lot of the bodies to see if there were drugs in their system. Many of the bodies had been cremated so this wasn't actually possible."

Traces of the same drug which Hoegel had used on Brigitte Arndt were found in 14 exhumed bodies.

In 2015, Niels Hoegel was convicted of three counts of murder, and two of attempted murder. At his trial, he had the attention he craved so much, but it was the wrong kind of attention.

"When he was brought in Niels H hid his face with a folder, and that wasn't remorse, that was probably because he doesn't like negative attention. This man has spent most of his adult life, it would seem, craving positive attention from being a hero. He's not being perceived as a hero at the moment and he would find that very difficult to deal with."

The police had strong suspicions that there were more victims than they had discovered, but while their investigations continued they satisfied themselves that Hoegel would be convicted for the deaths they could so far prove.

"While he was on trial, he started to talk with a forensic psychiatrist...a court appointed forensic psychiatrist, and this psychiatrist had already the feeling that he wanted to confess something. And he did. He told him that he injected this particular heart drug to 90 more patients at that hospital alone, and of those 90 patients, about 30 died. That was a big shock of course...so they started to exhume bodies."

Yet more bodies were exhumed – more heartache for many more families as their deceased loved ones were disturbed. Of course, this is exactly what the narcissistic Niels Hoegel wants, to keep himself in the spotlight, getting the attention he so desired.

"So, they had this massive investigation, they went through hundreds of medical records and looking for clues, because they couldn't just dig up hundreds of bodies and they realized that there were about 285 patients who had died during or shortly after his shifts. And of those 285, 101 were cremated and 184 were still buried. So, they went through their records again and they decided to dig up 99, and of those 99 I believe 27 showed traces of the heart drug he used."

The forensic psychiatrist had his work cut out for him. Niels Hoegel couldn't remember, or claimed he couldn't remember, any details of his victims, details which the police needed in order to further their investigations. Whether that was a ruse on Hoegel's part to perpetuate the attention, or whether he genuinely couldn't remember, is anybody's guess. The forensic psychiatrist had to work tirelessly in order to glean the necessary information from Hoegel.

He 'regressed' Hoegel to his time at the hospital, uncovering tiny details in order to stimulate his memories – details such as positioning of the beds, the windows, his signature on the medical records – anything which might bring Hoegel's mind back to each crime.

"He confesses to the 27 deaths they found in principal because he can only remember a few details which is very very odd but also if he has killed so many people, maybe, you know, you just don't remember all the details anymore."

Escalation

There is a phenomenon among serial killers known as the cooling off period, and at first Hoegel's cooling off period – that is, the time between killings -would last months. Criminologist Jane Monckton-Smith explains:

"When we talk about serial killers and the cooling off period, what we're talking about is their compulsion to kill, so the compulsion slowly gets stronger and stronger, if you think of it like a graph until we get to the peak, where they feel they need to kill, and they do that. And then they feel satiated and they start to come back down again, and this is why we see with serial killers quite a lot, that they can just return to normal after they have killed somebody, and we can't understand that...so while they're in this period of having cooled off, it starts to build again, and build again, and when it does build again they will be compelled to kill when they hit the top of that peak, and in this case it seemed that his need to kill was getting shorter and shorter, and so he was needing to kill more and more often."[20]

But was Ajmalin the only drug used by Hoegel in his killing spree? The police think not. On studying the number of deaths, it was found that he was suspected of killing more than once per shift – there were 50 double deaths (meaning two deaths occurred on one shift) and nine triple deaths (three deaths in one shift). Hoegel was present at 92% of the double deaths, and at all of the triple deaths and yet, Ajmalin could only be found in six of these cases, leading investigators to believe that the homicidal nurse employed more than one method of murder.[21] Police have pinpointed 5 different drugs which they say Hoegel used – Ajmalin, Lidocaine, Calcium Chloride, Amiodarone and Solatol, all of which cause heart arrhythmia and low blood pressure.

And So it Goes On

Hoegel is still being investigated, despite having already been jailed for life. As more and more evidence is uncovered, the story unfolds even more.

It is now believed that Hoegel first murdered a patient in February 2000, when he was still working at the Oldenburg clinic. It is also believed that he went on to kill around 35 more patients at the clinic before moving to Delmenhorst, where he was free to continue the stealthy slaughter of his patients. As the investigation into Nurse Niels Hoegel's crimes is set to continue, nobody knows how many patients he killed while pretending to care for them, although it is thought to be at least 90.

Hoegel isn't the only person to be held accountable for these deaths, however. Six members of staff from the Delmenhorst clinic are facing charges of manslaughter for their failure to intervene, and it seems likely that staff at Oldenburg Hospital will also be made to face the consequences of their inactions.

Remorse

A psychiatrist involved in the case told the court that Hoegel was full of remorse for the pain he had inflicted on the bereaved families, and, contrary to popular belief he was not 'basking in the limelight' of the case. "This is not so. He is deeply ashamed," [22]

But there are others who doubt his sincerity.

"He has expressed his remorse, he said he is honestly sorry for what he did, he hopes the families will find peace for the crimes he committed. But...he also said that it happened relatively spontaneous, which doesn't sound like taking on a lot of responsibility."[23]

As the German judicial system does not hand down consecutive sentences, any further convictions will not affect Hoegel's sentence[24], but it may bring some small relief to those families who have been in limbo, not knowing whether their loved ones died of natural causes or if they were, in fact, murdered.

Nurse Niels Hoegel craved attention – and that attention seems set to continue for many years to come.

SEE JANE KILL : THE GREATEST FEMALE SERIAL KILLER

AMY DEMPSEY

Jane Toppan

In 1887, a woman named Amelia Phinney was recovering from surgery for a uterine ulcer at Cambridge Hospital, Boston. Suffering pain from the procedure, she asked her nurse for something to ease the discomfort. The nurse, Jane Toppan, obliged, and although the medicine she gave to Amelia tasted foul, Jane encouraged her to finish it. As she drifted in and out of consciousness, she felt someone in the bed with her, kissing her face and caressing her. The attention suddenly stopped, and the following morning Amelia awoke and put the memories down to a strange dream. It wasn't until 1901, when Jane Toppan was arrested, that Amelia realised she had escaped the Angel of Death.

Her Early Years

Jane Toppan was born in Boston, Massachusetts, in 1857. Records about her early life are few and far between, but it is known that she was born Honora Kelley, the youngest of three daughters [2] (although some records show two daughters, and others suggest four) to Irish immigrants, Peter and Bridget Kelley. Bridget died of consumption (tuberculosis) when Honora was small, and Peter was left to raise his daughters alone. However, Peter was a chronic drunk. Known locally as 'Kelley the crack' (crackpot) for his eccentric and erratic drunken behaviour, [3] he was unable to cope with his daughters and in 1863 Peter placed his two youngest daughters, Honora and Delia, into the Boston Female Asylum, [4] an orphanage for orphans and destitute girls in Boston. [5]

When staff at the orphanage saw the poor state of the girls, they agreed to take them in. Peter Kelley later succumbed to insanity and was institutionalised for, allegedly, sewing his own eyelids together whilst working as a tailor. An older daughter, Nellie, was also reportedly institutionalised when she went violently insane in her twenties. [6]

The Toppans

In 1865, when Honora was only 7 or 8, she was taken in by the Toppan family as an indentured servant, meaning that she worked in service in return for bed, board, education and an agreed sum to be paid at the age of 18 when she would be released from her contract.

Although the family never formally adopted Honora, she took their last name and changed her first name to Jane. [8]

Jane excelled at school. She was described as 'brilliant and aggressive, and a leader of her class. She was also troubled, resorting to petty theft and lying. [9]

Jane's foster sister, Elizabeth, always treated her with kindness, but despite this, Jane's time with the Toppan family was not happy. Ann Toppan, the head of the household, treated Jane with disdain and made her feel ashamed of her Irish heritage. So much so, in fact, that she told friends that the young girl was an Italian immigrant whom the family had rescued from the streets.

Jane herself adopted this attitude, and in a bid to forget her own roots she would often be heard making disparaging remarks about other Irish people.

Ann Toppan was a cruel taskmaster and took every given opportunity to make her foster daughter feel small. As a result, Jane developed a personality which made her appear affable to others and was well-known for telling tall stories. But even this was ammunition for Mrs Toppan, as she attributed Jane's fondness for story-telling to the 'gift of the gab' – a talent for which the Irish were well-known. [10]

Despite Elizabeth's kindness, however, Jane developed an intense jealousy of her foster sister. Elizabeth was older by some years, and far prettier than 'plain Jane' and the younger girl envied Elizabeth's beauty and certain marriage.

These feelings were further compounded when, according to some reports, Jane was courted by a young man, an office worker from Lowell, when she was in her late teens. The relationship seemed to be going well when the young suitor gave Jane an engagement ring engraved with the image of a bird. Things turned sour, however, when the young man took a job in another town and fell in love with the daughter of his new landlord, and he called off the engagement. [11]

This betrayal proved to be a pivotal point in Jane's future behaviour, as she has been cited as saying "If I had been a married woman, I probably would not have killed all of those people. I would have had my husband, my children and my home to take up my mind." [12] Such was Jane's misery at being jilted, she began eating for comfort and gained a considerable amount of weight – at one point reaching 170lbs, which, on a diminutive 5'3" frame, is a lot of weight to carry. Her feelings of worthlessness grew, along with her resentment of the much-courted Elizabeth.

In 1874, Jane, by now 18, was released from her indenture and paid a lump sum of $50 (roughly $1064. 73 in today's money [13]) as per the terms of her contract. However, she decided to remain at the house in service to the family. Elizabeth married a young deacon of the local church, Oramel Brigham, and shortly afterwards her mother, Ann Toppan died, leaving everything to Elizabeth and nothing to her foster daughter, [14] a fact which further cemented Jane's resentment and loathing of her foster sister.

Jane stayed at the Toppan's house for a further ten years after she was released from her indenture. She was 28 when she eventually left in 1885. Although nothing is known about the circumstances of her departure – whether she was told to leave or left of her own free will – it is known that the ever gracious Elizabeth told Jane that there would always be a room at the house for her, should she wish to return. [14]

Nurse Jane

When Jane left the Brigham household, she decided to go into nursing, (one of only a handful of professions available to someone of Jane's social standing and gender), and began training at Cambridge Hospital in Boston.

Nurse Jane was a firm favorite among the patients – they loved her and nicknamed her 'Jolly Jane'. Her once maligned 'gift of the gab' stood her in good stead with the patients, who found her to be warm, attentive and caring.

Her co-workers, however, saw a vastly different side to their new colleague. She quickly became known as a liar and was wont to spread rumours about her colleagues and speak ill of people behind their backs to others. The rest of the staff quickly learnt not to trust the new trainee nurse.

Her professional ethics were also called into question when she was accused of stealing, and of altering patients' charts. Of course, Jane vehemently denied these accusations, and with no proof was allowed to continue with her training. [15] In actual fact, according to some sources, Jane's behaviour towards her fellow nurses, on occasion, led to a dismissal, and far from being dismayed that her antics had caused a colleague to lose her job, Jane would exhibit such extreme pleasure at their fate that it would alarm her fellow co-workers. [16]

The Angel of Death Emerges

It was during this time at Cambridge Hospital, that Jane began experimenting with her patients. At first, she would simply tamper with the patients' charts, or administer small amounts of medicine to the ones she liked to make them sick and prolong their stay. [17] However, as time went on this didn't appear to satisfy Jane's appetite for experimentation, and she began using her patients as guinea pigs in earnest, with deadly results. The small amounts of medicine used to induce sickness were no longer enough, and Jolly Jane turned to the drugs which were to become her hallmark – morphine and atropine.

To the Brink of Death

It is believed that in the beginning at least, Jane relied solely on morphine in her experiments. She would inject her chosen patient with the drug and stand back to watch the effects. The patient's pupils would contract, their skin would become clammy, and their breathing became laborious and loud. Depending on the dosage given, some of those patients would then slip into a coma, or even just stop breathing. Most satisfying to Jane, however, was when the patient would convulse, their body contorted with pain before they died.

On more than one occasion, Jane would take her patient to the brink of death before reviving them again, gaining a sense of professional pride in her life-saving skills. However, no matter how elated she felt having saved one of her victims' lives, nothing could compare to the thrill of seeing and feeling the life slip out of her target's body.

Soon, though, Jane had to add another ingredient to her deadly arsenal – atropine. Atropine is a fatal poison, derived from the belladonna plant, and was widely used in Victorian hospitals as a painkiller, as well as a go-to drug for many other conditions, such as whooping cough and tetanus. By introducing atropine to the mix, Jane could now witness (and enjoy) an entirely new set of effects. Pupils would dilate (rather than contract, as with the morphine), and patients would lose control of their muscles, often appearing intoxicated. The results would have been spectacular and gratifying for Jane to watch – her victims would sometimes laugh maniacally, or make low groaning sounds, much like that of a wounded animal. But possibly the most satisfying and exciting manifestation for Jane would be that of her patients pulling and plucking at objects around them, whether real or otherwise. Clothing, bed covers, their own fingers and toes – they would be compelled to pick continuously, even in their final moments, right up until death.

Jane was not content with merely administering the two drugs, though. She took great pleasure and interest in varying the dosages, watching the effects of the combinations. Her usual modus operandi seemed to be first injecting the patient with morphine and then, as they were about to lose consciousness, would offer them a glass of water with atropine dissolved in it. Sometimes, it seems, she would wait until the patient was near death from the morphine overdose, and then administer the atropine directly into the bowel by way of an enema, thus removing the last vestiges of dignity the patient might have left.

It is worth noting that Jane knew exactly what she was doing when using these drugs. Training of a nurse at that time was rigorous, to say the least. Much of it would have been what she had been used to in her years of service to the Toppans – cleaning, dusting, scrubbing floors and general 'housekeeping' of the wards for very little money, approximately $7 per month, out of which she had to buy all her books, as well as clothes and anything else she needed. But the training also included a weekly lecture on the medical profession and would have included the correct dosage and administration of drugs, of which morphine and atropine were just two. In fact, her final exam would have included questions on the correct dosage of atropine, morphine, and what should be done if a patient overdoses.

Jolly Jane Toppan knew exactly what she was doing.

There was more than one reason for Jane to use both atropine and morphine on her victims. Her first motivation was her own amusement. Jane got a huge thrill from watching her patients' reactions. She had a sadistic lust for their suffering and gained great pleasure from watching them writhe in pain before dying.

Her other reason for using the two drugs, however, was self-preservation. By using two substances which produced diametrically opposed reactions (morphine constricts the pupils, while atropine dilates them, for example), she could confuse the doctors who would examine the patients. In the absence of any textbook symptoms, the doctors would often attribute their deaths to a heart attack or diabetes. Jane would have derived a great deal of satisfaction from not only playing God with her patients but also from confounding the doctors. [18]

Sexual Thrill

Jane's perversion didn't stop at merely watching her patients suffer and die. Whilst it is not clear whether she sexually abused her victims, she later readily admitted to experiencing a sexual thrill from watching her patients dying, and this is borne out in the fact that she would climb into bed with them when they were close to death, pull them into her arms and hold them tight as the life drained out of their bodies. [19]

It was during this time that 36-year-old Amelia Phinney had her own brush with death at the hands of Nurse Jane. Amelia had had surgery for a uterine ulcer, a procedure which involved burning the ulcer with silver nitrate, and was recovering in bed at Cambridge Hospital. The post-operative pain she was experiencing made sleep impossible, and she became aware of someone standing by her bed. In the low light of the oil lamp, Amelia Phinney recognised her nurse, Jane Toppan, whose face, she recalled, had a look of deep intensity. Amelia asked Jane to fetch a doctor, as her pain was so bad, but Jane told her there was no need for a doctor, and she gave Amelia a drink, holding her up so she could sip.

Amelia did as her nurse told her, and shortly afterwards began to lose consciousness, but she later recalled that, through the haze, she felt the bedclothes being pulled back and another body joining her in bed. That body belonged to Jane Toppan, who proceeded to whisper to Amelia that everything would be alright. Amelia was powerless to move as the nurse caressed her, kissed her face, and peered excitedly into her eyes. The glass was once again brought to Amelia's lips as the nurse gently told her to drink some more, but the patient resisted and Jane suddenly left the bed and hurried from the room as though someone had disturbed her.

The next morning, when Amelia awoke, she put the bizarre happenings from the previous night down to a dream. [20]

Moving On

Although Jane was not liked by her colleagues, she had earnt the respect of some of the doctors at Cambridge Hospital, and, in order for Jane to further her studies, in 1888, they recommended her to the Massachusetts General Hospital.

Once again, Jane proved unpopular with her fellow nurses, who accused her of giving incorrect dosages to her patients. Talk was rife, with suspicions that several patients under Jane's care had died needlessly. However, it wasn't until the summer of 1890 that Jane was fired from her post at Massachusetts General, for leaving the ward without permission - a firm rule at the time.

Jane briefly returned to her job at Cambridge Hospital, but that was short lived as she was asked to leave because of reckless administration of opiates, a reputation which had dogged her career.

Private Nurse

In the summer of 1891, Jane decided to become a private nurse, and indeed she earned a reputation as the most successful private nurse in Cambridge. Her personality was not above reproach, however – her habit of telling lies and stealing continued and caused concern among some of her employers. Her free time did nothing to quash this reputation as Jane was known for drinking, and spreading rumours in her free time.

The Murders

Jane didn't need sick patients to murder, far from it. In fact, anyone who got in the way of what she wanted fell prey to the Angel of Death.

In 1895 Jane poisoned and killed Israel Dunham, her 77-year-old landlord because he was, according to her, feeble. Again, due to the complexities of her methods, doctors attributed his death to heart failure. Jane remained at no 19, Wendell Street, Boston, with Israel's widow, Lovey. However, by 1897 Jane had grown tired of her 'old and cranky' landlady. When the old lady fell ill in September of that year, Jane 'nursed' her, with her standard morphine and atropine. Lovey Dunham died.

1899 saw Jane claim two more victims. In the summer of that year, Jane stayed (as she had for several years) at a rented vacation home in Cataumet, Cape Cod. She had maintained a somewhat strained relationship (at least on her part) with her foster sister, Elizabeth Brigham, and that summer Jane invited Elizabeth to join her at the house. The pair had enjoyed a pleasant picnic, and on return to the house, Jane exacted her revenge. She mixed morphine with mineral water and gave it to her foster sister. However, Jane wanted Elizabeth, the foster sister she had resented for so many years, to suffer...a fact borne out years later when Jane confessed to her crimes, stating that Elizabeth was "really the first of my victims that I actually hated and poisoned with vindictive purpose." A quick death was not revenge enough for Jane, so she dragged the death out until finally, Jane climbed into bed with and held the dying woman as she took her last breath, later saying "I held her in my arms and watched with delight as she gasped her life out."

In December of that same year, a 70-year-old widow named Mary McNear was suffering from a cold and cough, having picked it up on Christmas day whilst visiting her daughter in Cambridge, who wasn't very well herself. Mary's family were concerned about her health and raised the idea of hiring a nurse to care for the elderly lady. The family's doctor, Dr Walter Wesselhoeft, however, deemed it unnecessary, saying that she only had a cold and their servant could administer everything she needed for her recovery – bed rest and hot tea. The family still felt a nurse was needed and asked Dr Wesselhoeft to recommend someone.

That someone was Jane Toppan.

Cheered and encouraged by the care and attention the nurse was bestowing on her Grandmother, Evelyn Shaw (Mary's granddaughter) returned home happy, but Mary's coachman arrived shortly after to tell her that Mary had passed out and could not be revived. Evelyn returned to her grandmother's house. The Dr was already there when she arrived and told Evelyn that Mary had suffered a stroke after receiving her medication. Nurse Toppan had informed the staff but told them there was no cause for alarm. The cook, though, took it upon herself to send the coachman to Evelyn's house despite Jane's assurances that all was well. The following morning, December 29th, 1899, Mary McNear passed away without having regained consciousness.

After the funeral, Mary's relatives discovered that some of Mary's best clothes were missing, and voiced their concerns to the doctor that the nurse may have stolen them. He, however, was furious at the suggestion and the family dropped the matter. [21]

Nothing and nobody would stand in the way of Jane getting what she wanted. February 1900 saw Jane's victimology take a new twist- the murder of a friend. Myra Connors was an old friend of Jane's and worked at the Theological School as a dining matron. Jane needed money, so she poisoned Myra with strychnine and took her job. Her position was short-lived, however, when Jane's stealing came to light and she was dismissed.

The Ones That Got away

Jane's next three victims escaped death at Jane's hands, but this was by design, and not luck on their part. In 1901, at the age of 44, Jane took up residence with new landlords, Melvin and Eliza Beedle. Never one to enjoy paying rent, Jane poisoned her landlords, but only enough to make them sick enough to need the help of a nurse. As she nursed them back to health, Jane turned her attention to the Beedle's housekeeper, Mary Sullivan. Jane poisoned Mary so that she fell unconscious and Jane brought it to the Beedle's attention that their housekeeper was a drunk. She was fired, and Jane took over her job, living rent free. [22]

The Beginning of the End

Jane's downfall began in the summer of 1901. For many years she had rented a holiday home in Cataumet from the Davis family, who owned a hotel there. Jane had been lax in paying her rent, and although she was a favoured guest, the Davis' decided that it was time to call in Jane's debt of $500 (approx. $13,500 today). In June, Mattie Davis travelled to Cambridge to visit Jane at the Beedle's house and collect her back rent. Jane offered Mattie some mineral water, laced with morphine, and when Mattie became sick Jane gave her some more of the drug. Over the course of seven days, Mattie became sicker and sicker as Jane continued to poison her, even doing so under the watchful eye of a doctor until, on July 5th, Mattie fell into a coma and died. [23]

Jane accompanied Mattie's body back home and was there at the funeral. The family was grateful to the nurse for caring for Mattie, and a week later she moved into the Davis house to look after Mattie's widower, Alden, who was beside himself with grief at the loss of his wife.

Over the following weeks, Jane started no less than three fires in the Davis' house in an effort to kill the rest of the family, but each attempt was dealt with swiftly, much to Jane's disgust.

On July 26th, only three weeks after Mattie's death, Jane poisoned Genevieve Gordon, the Davis' youngest daughter. Jane told the family that Genevieve had committed suicide because she could not bear the grief of losing her mother. The death certificate stated that it was a heart attack.

Less than two weeks after the death of his daughter, Alden Davis also died at the hands of Jane Toppan, which the doctor put down to a cerebral hemorrhage.

Jane asked the oldest daughter of the Davis family, Minnie Gibbs, to write off the $500 debt she owed to the family. Minnie refused. [24] On August 12th, 1901, Jane murdered Minnie by way of morphine tablets. In a particularly twisted act, as Minnie lay dying Jane brought Minnie's ten-year-old son into her bed with her. There is no way of knowing whether any sexual assault took place on the boy. [25]

Having wiped out the entire Davis family, Jane returned to Lowell in late August. She had her sights set on marrying Oramel Brigham,

her foster sister's widower. However, one person stood in her way –
Oramel's sister, Edna Bannister, 77, so Jane did what she always did, and
murdered her. She also poisoned Oramel himself, but only enough to
make him sick so that she could prove her love for him by nursing him
back to health. Nothing worked, and Oramel told Jane to leave, but not
before Jane herself made a suicide attempt of her own.

Jane's Arrest

On August 31st, 1901, Captain Gibbs (Minnie Gibbs'
father-in-law) ordered the bodies of the entire Davis family to be
exhumed, to see whether his suspicions of their murders could be
confirmed. By this time Jane had travelled to New Hampshire to stay
with an old friend, Sarah Nichols, but had read about the exhumations
in the newspaper.

On October 29th, 1901, Jane was arrested for the murder of
Minnie Gibbs, and on December 6th, 1901, Jane was formally charged
with four counts of murder – the entire Davis family.

Newspapers reported on March 31st, 1902, that Jane had
undergone a psychiatric evaluation and had been classed as insane. She
had admitted to the panel of experts that she had a sexual compulsion
to kill, and confessed to 11 murders.

The Trial

The trial of Jane Toppan opened on June 23rd, 1902. The entire
trial took less than eight hours, and the jury needed only 20 minutes to
deliberate and deliver the verdict of Not Guilty by reason of insanity.
She was sentenced to life at Taunton Insane Hospital, something she
seemed delighted at. She believed that she would be freed in a matter
of months because she would be able to convince the hospital that she
was not, in fact, insane.

It later emerged that Jane had confessed to her defense lawyer,
James Stuart Murphy, that she had committed more than 31 murders.
This confession was published in the New York Journal, including her
admission that she had duped the panel into thinking she was insane,

and that she felt very smug indeed at having outsmarted the experts. She also described the 'exquisite pleasure' killing had given her, and the lack of remorse she felt at the murders.

Jane laid the blame for the murders on the fiancé who had jilted her when she was in her teens, claiming "If I had been a married woman, I probably would not have killed all of those people. I would have had my husband, my children and my home to take up my mind."

Despite her belief that she would be freed, Jane Toppan spent the rest of her life at the asylum. Had she been freed, her killing spree would no doubt have continued – she is reported to have said that her only ambition in life was "to have killed more people...helpless people....than any other man or woman who ever lived."

Jane died on August 17th, 1938, at the age of 81. During the first two years in the asylum, her mental health was scrutinised, with many people asking why she was there as she appeared totally sane. There then followed a slow decline into insanity, with Jane often seen soothing other patients, crying out that they were dying, and trying to administer imaginary doses. Ironically, she became convinced that she herself was being poisoned and would stop eating, resulting in a dramatic weight loss. In a letter written to one of her doctors, she made reference to the 'poisonings':

"Taunton Lunatic Hospital, July 1, 1904.——"Doctor Stedman: I wish to inform you that I am alive, in spite of the deleterious food which has been served me. Many efforts have been made to poison me – of that I am very sure. I am thin and very hungry all the time. Every nerve is calling for food. Why can't I have help? I ate a pint of ice cream and four oranges Saturday and Sunday. (Signed) JANE TOPPAN

"NORAH KELLEY." [27]

In the end, Jane Toppan's deeds came back to haunt her.

KILLER NURSE

THE TRUE STORY OF CHRISTINE MALEVRE

Jessi Gorman

Christine Malèvre was praised for her actions, initially. The courageous nurse was a "champion of euthanasia" who had faced down her conscience and made the difficult choice to help end the suffering of patients who were elderly or terminally ill. She was thanked by the relatives of her patients and even the Health Minister himself – but this "angel of mercy" was eventually accused of being a serial killer.

This saintly nurse was revealed to be anything but when her case went to trial. She wasn't doing the right thing by putting her patients out of their misery, the court determined – instead, she was a deranged megalomaniac who found illness and death to be morbidly fascinating.

"I decided to put an end to their suffering."

During her time working at Mantes-la-Jolie, a hospital near Paris, Malèvre had so many patients die under her care that the rest of the hospital staff began referring to her as "The Black Widow." Since she started at the hospital in 1997, 83 patients had died on her shifts. In addition to the nickname, Malèvre's mounting body count attracted the attention of the hospital director – and in May of 1998, he took the case to a public prosecutor.

Malèvre was suspended from her job on the hospital's cancer ward as the investigation began. Her job was her life – and without it, she saw no reason to carry on. On May 6, 1998, she ran herself a bath and got in with her bathing suit on. With an overdose of sleeping pills making their way through her system, Malèvre had resigned herself to die.

Just one week earlier, she'd lost a patient on her shift, a 71 year old man named Jacque Gutton, who'd been suffering through the terminal stages of lung cancer. While Gutton was not expected to recover, he'd died much sooner than his doctors had predicted – and Malèvre was, perhaps, attempting to escape investigation as authorities looked into the circumstances surrounding the untimely death.

Unfortunately for Malèvre, she was still alive when she was found unconscious in the bathtub. She was taken to the hospital and admitted to a psychiatric ward – and wound up making a shocking admission as the investigation continued.

"I can't remember exactly," she said. "But I must have done this to dozens of people. I decided to put an end to their suffering."

Soft, pretty, and gentle

Malèvre had dreamed of being a nurse ever since she was a little girl. She'd developed an affinity for the profession thanks to an early introduction – her sister Celine suffered from intense earaches, and often, her mother called a nurse out to the home for treatment. Malèvre was fascinated by the woman, and described her as "so soft, so gentle, so pretty."

She'd be a nurse too, someday. Soft, pretty, and gentle.

As a girl, Malèvre had developed a very close bond with her grandmother. When she was just 18, her grandmother passed away – and the sight of her beloved gran's dead body propped inside of an open casket was something she never managed to recover from.

She was faced with death again soon after, while on a backpacking trip through the country of Peru. Malèvre had come across the body of a young man, dead on the side of the road. Her nursing training took her to Africa, where she did an internship to become a professional nurse by working at a health centre in the bush. During the early years of her training, Malèvre broke down while attending the medical examination of a corpse – a panic attack had overwhelmed her.

But eventually, Malèvre's discomfort with death slowly bloomed into a "morbid fascination," as it would be described later. She began pursuing work in palliative care, where she'd be able to be around death and illness all the time.

And, according to some, take her patients' lives into her own hands – acting not out of love, they claimed, but out of a desire for power and control.

"I had crossed an invisible border, and I had crossed it in silence, in a total loneliness, since it is prohibited," wrote Malèvre in her book, translated from French. "The force of this account will not leave anybody intact."

The Madonna of euthanasia

Initially, under questioning, Malèvre confessed to having helped at least 30 terminal cancer patients die over a period of just fifteen months, between February 1997 and May 1998. However, her story changed a few months later, and she claimed that she'd only administered lethal doses of morphine to just four suffering patients.

The case quickly opened a public debate about the ethics of euthanasia. While Malèvre was harshly condemned by the Catholic Church, others hailed her for her "mercy" – in particular, French campaigners who were actively seeking a more progressive stance on assisted suicide. In fact, MPs used the case to demand that parliament examine the issue.

Malèvre received 5,000 letters of support, which recognized her as a "Madonna of euthanasia."

While the media and the public seemed to have taken Malèvre's side, the formal investigation was well underway – looking into potential charges of manslaughter. After just eleven months, however, those accusations were upgraded by the investigating judge. Malèvre no longer faced charges of manslaughter, but of premeditated murder.

The final report pointed to eleven suspicious deaths, dating back to January of 1997. The alleged victims were all between 72 and 88 years of age, and all were in the final stages of terminal lung cancer. All were killed by an overdose of morphine or a lethal injection of potassium.

"These cases shatter the legend of Christine Malèvre as an angel of mercy, bringing relief to patients at the end of their life," said Alain Junillon, counsel for the prosecution.

Due to insufficient evidence, charges could not be pressed for four incidences, but the seven charges with enough evidence for a conviction carried a potential sentence of 30 years in prison. At the time, in 2000, Malèvre was just 30 years old.

"She was not the champion of euthanasia, as she wanted to be seen," said Olivier Morice, a lawyer who represented four families of patients who passed away between 1997 and 1998 while under Malèvre's care at the François-Quesnay hospital. "She should be regarded as a serial killer, rather than someone motivated by compassion."

Conclusions from two separate psychiatric evaluations described Malèvre as "a person without true compassion," someone with an insatiable desire to hold "a position of power" over her trusting patients. According to many of her colleagues at Mantes-la-Jolie, she was "obsessed" with death and illness – while others claimed the nurse was a talented student.

She was also described as showing "excessive devotion" to her terminally ill patients. Often, Malèvre would even insist on dressing her own patients, once they had passed away. Generally, this task is handled by other hospital staff, like nurse's aides – rarely would it be assigned to the nurse themselves. She also attended the funerals of many of her patients, which was inconsistent with usual practices.

Hospital patients under Malèvre's care were also found to be three times more likely to die, a statistical study reported. While it is certainly not unusual for high numbers of patients to die on a ward for treating the terminally ill, a 150 per cent greater probability of death was more than enough to arouse suspicion.

"She bluffed many people," Morice said, "but now, it's all over."

But according to Malèvre's lawyer, Charles Libman, no link had been established between the nurse's actions and the deaths of these patients. He argued that Malèvre should be cleared of all charges.

"Christine Malèvre is neither the Madonna of euthanasia or a serial killer," said Libman. "She is just a nurse who let her compassion rule her."

In addition, he argued, Malèvre had been under the influence of neuroleptic drugs. She claimed one of the four deaths she had confessed to had been "accidental."

Before 1999, even, it was readily accepted that Malèvre had been simply following orders – acting on requests from either her patients' families, or the terminally ill themselves. According to Malèvre, she was relieving her patients of their suffering since the French health system didn't provide sufficient accommodations for people who were terminally ill. But she'd done so without the knowledge of the hospital authorities.

"It would have been inhuman to have allowed the kind of suffering I witnessed," Malèvre said. "People accuse me of being too human, but, in my profession, you can't be too human."

After Malèvre came forward with a confession, the first such admission at that time in France, many other nurses and doctors were encouraged to speak out about their own struggles with similar issues. According to then Health Minister Bernard Kouchner, who had also worked as a doctor, healthcare professionals are often faced with distressing choices like what Malèvre had described.

"We should not make hasty moral judgments," he said.

"The one he'd made promise."

However, when a suit was filed against the nurse by families of the deceased, an investigation into the questionable deaths became necessary.

According to the investigating magistrate, Malèvre hadn't been accused of any wrongdoing by any of the relatives of her patients prior to the filing of the suit. It was also determined that the nurse had not been motivated by money, personal gain, or encouraged by any pro-euthanasia organization.

With no evidence of any criminal activity, the magistrate ordered that Malèvre be freed. Upon release, she underwent psychiatric treatment at a sanatorium outside of Paris, and then fled to a remote area of Normandy in an attempt to establish a new life as a packer.

Many bereaved relatives didn't become suspicious about the circumstances surrounding the deaths of their loved ones until months later. According to Alain Le Maout, whose wife Denise passed away in 1997 at Mantes-la-Jolie, Malèvre called him the morning of November 9, 1997, insisting that he come to the hospital immediately.

Then, he claimed, Malèvre placed a call to the resuscitation unit at the hospital. Once she had described the symptoms Denise was supposedly experiencing, Malèvre told him she was directed to administer an injection that would ease his wife's minor epileptic fit.

"At 10 o'clock, when I arrived, Denise had just enough energy to turn to me and smile before she died in my arms," remembered Le Maout, who believes Malèvre had possibly given his wife a lethal dose of morphine.

Following the death of his wife, Le Maout received an interesting piece of mail – an invitation to Malèvre's upcoming wedding. A friend of his, who had lost her husband at the same hospital under similar suspicious circumstances, reached out to him.

"When she told me that she had also been invited to the wedding, I asked myself, 'Since when have nurses invited to their weddings widows and widowers of people who died in their care?'" Le Maout said.

His suspicions were heightened when he learned that Malèvre was working on a book about euthanasia, which graphically detailed the heart wrenching anguish of dying patients.

"I helped a human being to die because he'd asked me," wrote Malèvre in her book. "Was I a coward, was I weak? Who was I, this nurse who dared to hold the hand of a dying man and to shorten his suffering? I was the one he'd made promise. I was the one who helped him through his anguish."

The title of the book, My Confession, made Le Maout even more curious about what exactly happened on the morning of his wife's death. To this day, Malèvre has not addressed the circumstances of Denise's passing on November 9, 1997.

"When the moment arrives, we should not be alone."

Some hospital officials have attempted to account for Malèvre's behaviour, claiming she may have been affected by an incident involving a 76 year old woman who had been suffering from Alzheimer's disease. In March of 1996, Malèvre witnessed the patient's husband shoot her dead on the ward before taking his own life.

He'd left a letter behind, claiming he could no longer bear to see his wife in such condition.

"I feel great compassion for this nurse, who must not be made to feel alone and lost, like so many sick people isolated and cloistered in wards where people are watching them die," said then Health Minister Bernard Kouchner, when Malèvre was initially detained in 1998.

He added, however, that euthanasia was "unacceptable" under French law – despite admitting that the topic of mercy killing was "neither discussed enough nor taken seriously enough" in the country. While he felt doctors should not prolong the lives of suffering patients against their will, Kouchner said active euthanasia was "a barbaric word."

According to a French spokesman for the Roman Catholic church, healthcare providers in France were subject to a "legal vacuum" – without clarified, specific regulations to dictate exactly how these caregivers, including doctors and nurses, should support the terminally ill through the final phases of their lives.

Even painkilling therapy was underdeveloped in France, Kouchner said. The country's social security budget at the time lacked appropriate funding for "palliative care teams," which he said was contributing to a serious issue within French hospitals.

"We need them, because a third of our population will soon be in retirement," he explained. "We are all mortal, and when the moment arrives, we should not be alone."

Doctors in many countries can follow strict protocol and allow their patients the right to die under certain conditions, granting them freedom from prosecution. However, in France, the word 'euthanasia' does not even appear within the penal code, and the subject itself is considered quite taboo. Active euthanasia, according to French law – the act of administering a substance which will likely hasten death – is treated as murder.

Another former French Health Minister, Dr. Jean-François Mattei, has also spoken out strongly in opposition to the practice, describing it as "the wrong answer to questions of suffering, solitude, and abandonment."

Still, a report released by France's National Ethics Committee indicated that the practice was already being practiced at many of the country's hospitals – although the "carefully worded" document was not a push for updated legislation. In 1995, a survey conducted among 140 French anaesthetists revealed that 26 per cent had purposefully injected patients with lethal drugs "when they felt that the patients had no chance of recovery."

Additionally, a French poll from December 2002 revealed that 88 per cent of respondents were in support of legalizing euthanasia under certain conditions. Even Le Maout admitted he can see the necessity of assisted suicide.

"I am not opposed to euthanasia," he said. "In fact, my wife, her doctor, and myself considered it a possibility if her illness became too painful to bear."

Denise's condition had been improving prior to her death, though – raising even more suspicion. Le Maout said he hoped to see Malèvre face a maximum penalty for her role in the deaths of many innocent patients.

"Knowing she is still at liberty, after admitting involvement in four deaths and being accused of seven murders, revolts me," he said. "I am fundamentally non-violent, but today I cannot say what I would do if by chance I came face to face with Christine Malèvre."

Self-centered motives

But Malèvre's actions were not entirely unusual. In fact, terms like "Code Blue killers" and "Mother Teresa syndrome" came about to describe health care workers who use sympathy and compassion as an excuse to overdose their victims and relieve their suffering. While many of these killers claim they only did it because they thought they were helping, there are likely more – possibly including Malèvre herself – who kill because of other motivations.

According to a former nurse named Paula Lampe, who has done extensive case studies and detailed research into health care serial killers, Mother Teresa syndrome occurs when a caregiver looks past the needs of their patients. Instead, these individuals begin to focus on their own needs – and develop an addiction to the feeling of being needed.

The effect is similar to the early stages of falling in love, she added.

"This syndrome ranges from excessive self-sacrifice to outright aggression, all in the name of meeting one's personal need for love and attention," explained Katherine M. Ramsland in her book, Inside the Minds of Healthcare Serial Killers: Why They Kill.

Sufferers of this syndrome, Ramsland wrote, tend to be meticulous, reliable, and competent workers – but are also typically loners who may choose to isolate themselves. Some might also struggle with anger management issues, and could see weakened patients as easy targets to work through their aggressions.

"Victims are readily available, and it's not that difficult to cover up certain types of murders in a major hospital – especially if the patients are elderly, very young, or suffer from serious illnesses or injuries," Ramsland wrote in the introduction to her book.

However, not all health care killers are specifically looking for potential victims. Ramsland explained that for others, it's an escape from a typically dull existence. While most of the killers initially attempt to defend their actions by claiming they were trying to help their suffering patients, Ramsland said that in most cases, evidence later reveals that they "clearly had other motives – mostly self-centered."

"After saving a patient, they experience an emotional high – and some nurses then start putting patients at risk so they can achieve the adrenaline rush again," states Ramsland. "When life gets hard or boring, especially, they seek ways to invigorate it."

Ramsland also noted that experts who have investigated killings within the health care industry speculate that physicians, nurses, or hospital support staff have "contributed more serial killers than all other professions combined." An especially disturbing fact as these individuals have all taken an oath to do no harm as they provide necessary care to those in life's most vulnerable conditions.

Some experts even believe that the type of crime that is generally committed by health care workers – which includes abuse, assault, exploitation, neglect, fraud, and murder – is an indication of the direction crime is generally moving.

"It's an interpersonal crime, and it's definitely happening in the health care workplace," said health care expert Beatrice Yorker, who published an examination of health care serial killers in the Journal of Forensic Science. "With a body count over 2000, just of convicted health care killers, that is as high as non-health care serial murderers. It's a significant issue, and it warrants significant resources to address and resolve."

Yorker's study determined that the majority of health care killings were generally committed in the same way Malèvre had caused the deaths of her terminal patients – through the lethal injection of narcotics like epinephrine, insulin, anectine, digoxin, KCL, pavulon, or lidocaine. One of the key ways a poisoning differs from other kinds of killings is that it is very obviously a premeditated act, one which requires careful planning and is rarely committed in the heat of the moment.

And, according to forensic science expert Kathy Steck-Flynn, the terminally ill are especially vulnerable to poisoning – and health care professionals have easy access to the drugs required to commit such a crime.

"Perpetrators of homicidal poisonings are often employed in the medical or caregiving fields," she wrote. "Though there are no proven theories to explain this phenomena, perhaps their behaviour is similar to that of pedophiles, who often take on roles in positions of trust over children, such as coaches, clergy, and other professions, in order to gain access to their victims.

"Poisoners, in some cases, take on jobs that give them access to poisonous substances – and having poisons (or drugs) in ready reach and extensive knowledge of their effects may be what tempts perpetrators to use them in a crime."

However, Ramsland said that not all health care killers specifically enter the industry with the intent of preying on easy victims. She added that while she feels that some killers may be mentally ill or compulsive, she doesn't believe that they are insane – "I don't think they could get into their positions if they were actually psychotic."

"Many transform into killers on the job," she noted. "After killing once, usually out of pity, they learn that they enjoy it – and so they continue."

Ramsland has identified other potential motives, including the desire to be a hero, seeking attention, experimenting with drugs and therapies, or even sexual arousal.

According to researchers who have investigated serial killers in nursing, many appear to display a "pathological interest in the power of life or death" – exactly what Malèvre's co-workers described noticing in the nurse's behaviour. But Ramsland said often, those who go on to become health care serial killers might not be attracted to actually committing murders "until they actually find themselves in a situation where they can exercise some power."

Still other researchers argue that many health care murder cases aren't as clear-cut as other situations – can "mercy killings" really be considered serial murder?

"Nurses kill because they believe in euthanasia," stated Theodore Dalrymple, who has written extensively about the topics of murder, euthanasia, and the culture surrounding both. "In a culture as fixated on youth as our own, old age is seen in itself as something terrible, cruel, pointless, and even obscene ... The helpless are often not very appealing – it is all too easy to think the world would be better off without them."

The end of a dream

On January 30, 2003, following a four-hour deliberation, Malèvre was handed down a prison sentence of ten years for the murder of six of her hospital patients and ordered to pay 92,910 euros to the families of her victims. Malèvre was acquitted of the seventh count, and was also banned from continuing to practice nursing or work in the health care industry at all.

Prosecutors had pushed for ten years as a minimum sentence – still too lenient a punishment for the severity of her crimes, according to the families of many of Malèvre's victims. Under French law, she could have faced a potential life sentence.

"If Christine Malèvre had been tried for killing seven people in good health, we'd be far from ten years and closer to life in prison," said Morice. "(She) is a woman who is unbalanced and who deliberately overstepped her authority."

According to Elizabeth Bryant, who covered the trial for United Press International, Malèvre sat "stony-faced" as the verdict was read, but was in tears before the sentencing was over.

"But I want to live," Malèvre sobbed to the court. "I want to start a family."

Malèvre was released in 2007, although an appeals court had increased her sentence to twelve years just a few months after her trial. It seems her dream to have a family of her own came true – she fell in love and got married. But the little girl who'd always wanted to be a nurse would have to settle for work as an accountant, since she would never again be able to work at a hospital.

Even with the verdict against Malèvre, pro-euthanasia activist organizations have used the case as an example of why the practice should be legalized. According to a United Press International article by Elizabeth Bryant, the trial "helped highlight the problem of clandestine mercy killings" – something activists argue is a too-frequent occurrence at many French hospitals.

"It's exactly this type of action we are fighting against," said Edith Deyris, secretary general of the Paris-based Association for the Right to Die in Dignity. "We want transparency. We want a realization and concerted action within hospitals – based on written demands of patients who want to die."

"In other words," Deyris added," the complete opposite of the shadows and impreciseness we found ourselves with the trial of Christine Malèvre."

As of January 2017, euthanasia remains against the law in France – and while it seems the number of health care serial killers seems to be growing, researchers agree that there are still more good doctors and nurses than there are bad ones.

"That some doctors become killers says much about human nature, society, and the practice of medicine," said forensic psychiatrist Robert Kaplan. "But it should be remembered that very, very few members of a great profession follow this path – the practice of medicine is an inherently good activity."

SERIAL KILLER DOCTOR : THE TRUE STORY OF ALICE WYNEKOOP

NATHAN NIXON

The Wynekoop Case

There are few murder cases in history that have been as bizarre as The Wynekoop case. Perhaps it is the circumstance of a mother allegedly committing an awful act for her son that grabbed so much attention. Maybe it was the sense among American's that such a seemingly sweet and noble woman could not possibly have committed such a crime. During a time in the United States that is already a tale of struggle and recovery, this murder set in 1933 stood in the headlines for weeks and gripped an entire class of people along the way. The story of Dr. Alice L. Wynekoop is one for the ages.

Alice Lindsay was born in 1870. Although little was recorded or known of her early life, it is well documented that she lived an absolutely normal childhood. The importance of The Wynekoop case begins with her marriage to Frank Wynekoop in the 1890's. Alice Lindsay took the famous name, now, of Alice Lindsay Wynekoop. She worked hard in her education in the medical field, and soon became a full practicing doctor in the late 1890's. By the turn of the century, Dr. Alice Wynekoop, along with her husband Frank Wynekoop, would start to put together the foundation for what would later become one of the Chicago area's most chilling scenes.

The beginning of this chilling case actually begins in 1901. Frank and Alice Wynekoop decided to supervise the construction of a massive red-bricked mansion in the west side of Chicago. Their thinking was to create a safe, family centered environment for their entire family. Soon after, the property was popularly said to be "cursed". Frank and Alice had several children. Their daughter, Marie Louise, died there inside the home in an upstairs bedroom. Frank's brother, Dr. Gilbert Wynekoop, put the entire family in the headlines when he attempted to strangle his unfaithful wife during their divorce proceedings. This was said to have happened in the family living room. Dr. Gilbert Wynekoop later was clinically diagnosed as insane and was institutionalized.

All of these dreadful event happened in a 20 year timespan leading up to the dreariest event of them all. Before the murder, the house was already tagged as haunted throughout the neighborhood. The Wynekoop's were ultimately the black sheep of the neighborhood. It is important to keep in mind the era that this is in. This was a time in American History when the totality of medical care was transitioning to major hospitals and medical establishments. There was still, however, significant medical care that was happening in local housing. The Wynekoop household fit this bill. They had several rooms in the house devoted to the family medical practice. There were rooms for operations and general care as well as a morgue in the basement. This was obviously well known in the neighborhood, and gave more material for the whispers around town to gossip about. Those whispers gained a much bigger voice in 1933.

Prior to 1933, there was actually some positivity toward Dr. Alice Wynekoop. While many spoke of the property being haunted and many in the neighborhood holding a genuine fear of going around the house, that opinion was not generally shared in regards to Frank and Alice Wynekoop. Dr. Alice Wynekoop was an influential figure in the women's suffrage movement as well as an advocate for women's rights as a whole. Alice graduated medical school from Northwestern University in Illinois. She was generally admired and held in high regard for her medical practicing in the area. She would commonly provide medical care to those in need when they may not have had the means to garner medical attention from other places. She was a one of the primary leaders in the evolution of child healthcare and believed wholeheartedly in fair, honest medical treatment of everyone, regardless of their income or ability to pay. For these reasons, the bizarre events of 1933 still have people split on what really happened. Dr. Alice Wynekoop, for all intents and purposes, could also be called a killer and a liar.

The relationship that Alice had with her son is of supreme importance to the case. Frank and Alice's son, Earle Wynekoop, was generally described as a low-life. Specifically, he desired to stay in the mansion as long as possible. He often leeched money off of Alice and Frank and was never really forced to grow up.

In 1929, Dr. Frank Wynekoop, the husband of Alice Wynekoop, passed away. This left the massive 16 bedroom mansion with only Alice Wynekoop, Earle Wynekoop, and Rheta Wynekoop, the wife of Earle.

Earle and Rheta Wynekoop had an unsuccessful marriage to say the least. After her death, a deep investigation was conducted by investigators into the past of Earle Wynekoop. Earle was said to have a "black book" with as many as 50 names in it. He frequented fairs, where he would set out to woo as many women as he could. He famously is said to have had "as many as 25 fiancée's" at one point in time. Many women who would later be questioned said that "he made love to them in the strangest and most repulsive ways." This would all lead to Rheta Wynekoop questioning their marriage. Rheta grew tremendously depressed and often times found herself in competition with Earle's lovers. She famously weighed herself as much as ten times per day.

Although Earle had fallen out of love with Rheta shortly after their honeymoon, the marriage continued in the oddest of circumstances. In 1933, the Wynekoop mansion housed Alice, Earle, Rheta, and a boarder or little significance to the case. The basement of the mansion was the site of great medical care as well as several other bedrooms in the house. This was an odd living situation for all involved.

Dr. Alice Wynekoop tried all that she could to support the marriage. Strangely enough, this repulsed Rheta even more. Rheta felt that Alice had "blind support" for Earle, regardless of what he did and how he did it. To supremely set the stage for baffling case, Alice had taken up life insurance policies on Rheta just weeks before her tragic death. Upon the death of Rheta Wynekoop, Alice was set to collect

$12,000, a staggering amount of money in the depression era in the early 1930's.

The overall situation of the Wynekoop's was a bit strange. With all of these things considered, it is no wonder how there could be reasonable suspicion raised about Dr. Wynekoop's part in a heinous crime. The events of the murder are both chilling and confusing. The night of November 21, 1933 will forever be an event that still has many questions surrounding it.

The Murder

It was around 10 P.M. that a police officer that was out on patrol was dispatched to the Wynekoop home. Who was the person who phoned police on that evening? Ironically enough, the caller was none other than Dr. Alice Wynekoop.

"Something terrible has happened," Dr. Alice Wynekoop said to police upon entering the home. "Come on downstairs and I will show you."

Officers would describe Alice Wynekoop as anxious and jittery. The officer notably referenced a calm in her voice, however.

The group made their way downstairs to the doctor's operating room in the Wynekoop home. Immediately upon entering the room, it was quickly clear that something wasn't quite right.

On a table in the center of the room lay a body. The body was still slightly warm to the touch and showed evidence of very recent death. A sheet had been thrown over the body, leaving only bare feet and the head and upper shoulders exposed. The face had numerous scratches on it, however nothing specifically deep or significant. There was moderate bruising over many parts of the body as well as discoloration on several areas of the flesh. It appeared as if there was some sort of struggle that took place before the body was placed on the table. This was the body of Rheta Wynekoop, wife of Earle Wynekoop and daughter in law off Dr. Alice Wynekoop.

Upon further examination of the body, it was quickly discovered that Rheta had suffered a gunshot wound through the back. With closer examination, the bullet was tracked to have entered the back just above the midline and to have taken an upward course through the torso. The bullet was lodged just beneath Rheta's left breast. After autopsy, the final exam would show that the entire thorax was filled with blood. The overall significance to investigators with this information was that it showed Rheta was alive when she was shot. This indicated that the official cause of death was the gunshot wound to her back causing hemorrhage and shock. The manner of death was officially ruled a homicide.

Autopsy also revealed a significant level of chloroform. Chloroform held many important medicinal uses, especially in the 1930's. A common anesthetic, chloroform was a popular choice among doctors as an agent to administer prior to a surgery. Investigation of the scene found a bottle of chloroform in the operatory room where Rheta was found. It was almost completely empty.

Also found at the crime scene was a revolver. The revolver showed signs that it had just been fired. There were also three displaced cartridges next to the revolver. This would prove to be the murder weapon. Oddly enough, the revolver belonged to Earle Wynekoop.

Earle Wynekoop would seem to have been a prime suspect upon the initial discovery of the body of Rheta. After all, he was in a marriage that he had no interest in being in. He had countless instances of unfaithfulness to support this theory. Rheta was unhappy with the marriage as well, as she knew of his acts outside of their marriage.

Earle Wynekoop was not at the house at the time of the murder according the Dr. Alice Wynekoop and others at the scene. Police questioned Earle and this statement was supported. Earle Wynekoop was driving to Arizona at the time of the murder. This led investigators to quickly eliminate him as a suspect in the murder. Dr. Wynekoop's daughter did not live in the house hold. She was a physician at Cook County Hospital. While Dr. Alice Wynekoop's daughter was present at the home at the time of the murder, it was professed to authorities by Alice Wynekoop that she was only asked for help after the body was discovered. Enid Hennessey, who was renting out a room at the house, was not accounted for at the time of the murder. She was quickly ruled out as a suspect as she had no connection to the family nor the murder beyond maintaining a temporary living arrangement.

This left only Dr. Alice Wynekoop as a suspect. Police initially marked her as the prime suspect being as she apparently identified the body first. According to Alice's initial information that she gave to police on scene, the other members of the household had no contact with Rheta and couldn't have possibly been involved.

Police quickly got a statement from Alice Wynekoop as to what happened that evening. This is truly where things get complicated in this case. Dr. Alice Wynekoop's first statement was, perhaps, a far-fetched effort to lead investigator's down a winding road that could not necessarily be disproven.

According to the first statement, Dr. Alice Wynekoop entered the operatory at precisely 8:30 P.M. to "obtain some medicine for flu-like symptoms for both her and Enid." As she arrived in the room, she saw Rheta lying on the table. Alice examined her and confirmed that she was dead. It was at this time that Dr. Alice Wynekoop called her daughter at the hospital and notified her of what happened. Catherine Wynekoop quickly came home from the hospital and pronounced Rheta dead.

It was at this time that a red flag was apparent to investigators. Rather than immediately notify police of what happened, Dr. Alice Wynekoop instead chose to call an undertaker.

Alice Wynekoop was questioned as to who could have committed this murder if all was true as she said. Dr. Wynekoop blamed the murder on thieves. She explained that there had been numerous instances that her home was broken into by thieves who were out to collect money and drugs from her operating rooms down stairs.

Police found this all to be quite misleading. If she indeed suspected that Rheta had been murdered by thieves in an apparent break in, why would she not call authorities upon discovering Rheta's body?

The deck was beginning to stack against Dr. Wynekoop. Police questioned her a second time a few days later. She gave a nearly identical statement that featured even more details of how she discovered the body. She attempted to explain to authorities that even if she had notified authorities, Rheta was already dead when she found her. This still, however, baffled police. Moreover, extensive crime scene investigation of all of the downstairs offices of the Wynekoop home showed that there was no evidence of a burglary and there was nothing that was missing to provide evidence of a burglary. This left everything pointing still toward Dr. Alice Wynekoop as the murderer of Rheta Wynekoop.

For all of these extensive reasons, police arrested Dr. Alice Wynekoop and charged her with the murder of her daughter-in-law, Rheta Wynekoop. It was at this time that Alice gave the chilling statement that would be used at trial. The statement she would give was a completely irrational argument that defied belief. This third official statement has long been seen as one of the most erratic and random stories to explain a crime in recent history.

Dr. Alice Wynekoop would go into detail about some of the habits of Rheta.

"Rheta was greatly concerned about her health and her overall appearance," Alice said in her statement. "She was always weighing herself, usually stripping down to the nude in order to do so. On Tuesday, November 21, after a luncheon, at about 1:00 P.M. she decided to go into town to buy some sheet music that she had long been wanting."

Police immediately knew that this was going to work its way into a confession. The statement was carefully taken. It was during the opening parts of her confession that police noticed that her story was already changing dramatically from anything she had stated before.

"Rheta had decided to weigh herself before she headed into town. I was working in the operatory. She was sitting on the table, practically naked. She complained that she had pain in her side that was causing much more trouble than usual. I remarked to her that since it was a convenient time during the month for an examination of this kind, we should just as well conduct it."

"She was complaining of considerable pain and tenderness throughout the beginning of the examination," Wynekoop said.

It was at this time that the initial problem began according to Dr. Alice Wynekoop. Alice stated that she suggested some Chloroform be used to make the exam go easier. Dr. Wynekoop then prepared a Chloroform solution that Rheta self-administered using a medicinal sponge.

"She took several deep, slow inhalations of the sponge," Wynekoop said. "I continued my exam and asked her if I was hurting her. She gave no answer."

Dr. Alice Wynekoop continued with her confession. She admitted that when Rheta failed to provide any sort of answer after the Chloroform had been given, she examined her at once. She determined that her breathing had stopped. She administered CPR and artificial respiration techniques immediately for roughly 20 minutes, with no success. Alice Wynekoop examined her fully with a stethoscope, and no heartbeat was revealed. For all intents and purposes, she was officially dead at this point.

The next part of the confession is where things get extremely complicated. At this point in the confession, investigators tend to think that this could be a reasonable instance of doctor error. Assuming what she was confessing at this point were true, she could realistically have been charged with negligent manslaughter. It was what she would continue on to say that baffled investigators and opened the door for conspiracy theories by many.

"I wondered what action could best ease the situation for everyone involved," Dr. Alice Wynekoop went on to confess. "The presence of a loaded revolver seemed to offer the answers that I was seeking. Further injury was now impossible. With great difficulty, I exploded one cartridge at a distance of some half dozen inches from the patient. The gun dropped from my hand."

"The scene was so overwhelming. No action was possible for a period of several hours," She continued.

With this confession, police had all of the evidence that they needed to charge and convict their prime suspect of first-degree murder. Prosecutors were able to use this third statement as confession and admit it to the court room during trial. Although there were many questions that were unanswered, the jury quickly found Dr. Alice Wynekoop guilty of first-degree murder. She was sentenced to 25 years in prison. Being as how she was 62 years old at the time of conviction, this sentence basically was a life sentence.

Assuming that the confession given by Dr. Alice Wynekoop were true, it left a mess of unanswered questions that the defense team tried to use in the court room.

The most pressing question was an obvious one. Alice Wynekoop admitted to firing the shot that killed Rheta Wynekoop. The issue with this is, however, is that she admitted to only one shot. There were three displaced cartridges at the murder scene. The mystery surrounding the other two shots has long been unsolved, as only one bullet was confirmed to have entered into Rheta's body. Many suggest that perhaps Dr. Alice Wynekoop was set to commit suicide, but couldn't keep the gun nestled out of fear. This is just a theory obviously, but no real answer has ever come about.

When police initially came to discover the body of Rheta Wynekoop, it was noted that she had significant amounts of bruising on her body. The bruising was not isolated to one spot. There was discoloration noted on numerous parts of her body. Along with bruising and discoloration were scratches. There were several noticeable scratches to her face and neck area. There wasn't a single part of Dr. Alice Wynekoop's confession that explained these marks. There was no part of the confession that talked of even the slightest struggle. This has long led many to speculate that Rheta was never murdered in the operatory room. A wide belief by many is that the murder happened elsewhere outside of the home. Chloroform was used to make her lose consciousness and she was later shot to finish the job. The bruising and scratches would be evidence that there was a struggle to get her to inhale the Chloroform. The further bruising would show signs of the unconscious body being moved from several locations. This has widely been an accepted theory, especially by those who believe that Earle Wynekoop was really the murderer.

Many wondered what would push an otherwise rational, humanely practicing doctor to commit such a heartless, inhumane act. Police admittedly were shocked at the confession and wondered how she could have gotten to this point. Perhaps the most widely accepted conspiracy theory that has come about with this case is the mother-son conspiracy. This theory is based off of the thought that Dr. Alice Wynekoop could not have possibly committed such a heinous crime. This theory goes into detail about how Earle Wynekoop was stuck in a marriage that was only bringing him misery. Earle also was vastly unsuccessful and freeloading off of his mother. After pressure from both Rheta and his mother, he was at his end with the pressure of it all.

The theory goes to say that Earle Wynekoop shot Rheta Wynekoop in the back outside of the home. He then loaded her body into his car and took her to the Wynekoop home. Upon getting the body into the operatory room, Dr. Alice Wynekoop determined her to be dead. Alice

Wynekoop had an unbreakable love for her son. She quickly came up with a plan to take blame for the murder so that her son would not get in trouble. Earle Wynekoop was then told by Alice to get in the car and start driving before she called to notify police. This would give him an alibi. It was now that she tried to frame herself for the murder and planned her story.

While there are several details added and taken away depending on who you are hearing this theory from, the basis of it is a simple concept. In criminal history, this sort of murder that the theory suggest is quite common. Essentially, a husband or wife wants out of a marriage. To them, murder is an option to get out of the marriage and save reputation and money.

To take this theory even a bit further, many suggest that perhaps Earle and Alice even planned the murder. This is how some explain Dr. Alice Wynekoop taking out the life insurance policy on Rheta for $12,000. While the defense team argues that this is merely a coincidence, it is hard to ignore the timing of that with the murder.

Yet another detail from the confession that didn't make any sense to investigators was the cause of death. Dr. Alice Wynekoop confessed that the Chloroform was what, in fact, killed Rheta Wynekoop. She admitted that she shot Rheta in the back only after she was dead in an effort to perhaps escape persecution. This in itself doesn't make much sense, but when this is coupled with the coroner's report, is just plain false. The blood found in the thorax of Rheta Wynekoop proves that she was alive when she was shot in the back. This is another red flag that many see as more evidence that points to Alice Wynekoop making up a story to cover for someone.

There has also been shaky evidence of the exact whereabouts of Earle Wynekoop on the day of the murder. While Alice Wynekoop stated that he had left on Sunday for his business trip to Arizona, it was confirmed by Stanley Young of Chicago, a nephew of E. Q. Johnson, former United States District Attorney, that Earle and Alice

Wynekoop had a secret meeting on Tuesday morning at 8:00 A.M. This is considered highly odd in any circumstance. Moreover, it is incredibly suspicious that Earle Wynekoop was emphatic about not notifying Rheta that he was still in Chicago.

Stanley Young confirmed that Earle was in Chicago on the day of the murder. While Earle would soon be on the road on the day of the murder, this makes it entirely feasible that something could have happened that morning and he left town to gain an alibi by the time the crime was reported.

Throughout this entire case, police felt like things just didn't add up. Initially, they felt like they had their suspect in Dr. Alice Wynekoop. When Alice Wynekoop ultimately confessed to the entire thing, things still just didn't quite add up to all involved.

Typically, an investigation is centered on the testimony of a suspect who is trying to prove their innocence. The suspect will contort the truth and tell a fabricated statement in a way that will prove they had nothing to do with the crime. Most often, these false statements are quickly picked through by investigators and the truth comes to the surface based on hard evidence and the work of many. This case, however, seems like the opposite happened. Years later, it became more apparent that Dr. Alice Wynekoop was likely not the murderer of Rheta Wynekoop. The puzzling part of the entire case though is that she seemingly lied and fabricated a story in an effort to be found guilty. While everyone could see the obvious flaw in her testimony, she put herself in a position to be found guilty. Whatever really happened on November 21, 1933 in that Chicago neighborhood will never actually be known. This will always be remembered as a case that found the guilty seemingly lying to go to jail.